A TREASURY of HYMN STORIES

Brief
Biographies
of 120
Hymnwriters
with Their
Best Hymns

AMOS R. WELLS

BAKER BOOK HOUSE
Grand Rapids, Michigan 49516

D0967443

Copyright © 1945 by Baker Books
a division of Baker Book House Company
P.O. Box 6287, Grand Rapids, MI 49516-6287

Reprinted 1992

Originally published under the title *Treasure of Hymns.*

ISBN: 0-8010-9718-5

Third printing, November 1993

Printed in the United States of America

Preface

THE present renaissance in hymn study and the discerning selection and use of hymns are evidenced in the republication of articles in this field that still retain accuracy, freshness and appeal. Dr. Amos Wells (1862–1933), famed as the managing editor of the *Christian Endeavor World*, also of Peloubet's Notes on the Sunday School lessons, and some sixty other books, member of the Appalachian Mountain, Twentieth Century, Browning, and Boston City Clubs, and a key man in the Federal Council of Churches, was ever a dynamic speaker and forceful consultant at conventions, conferences and educational institutions. A professor of Greek and geology at Antioch College, his academic training led him down the trunk lines of history, biography, literature, science, religion, and youth nature and nurture.

This TREASURE OF HYMNS evolved from ten years of editing hymn mosaics, one per month, for the *C. E. World*. Dr. Wells' style is simple, forceful, and prophetic in his inclusion of hymns, little known and unsung thirty years ago. America, the Beautiful, for example, written in 1893, revised in 1910, with the tune Materna not even a distant cousin, is here graphically pictured, with a humorous snapshot of Katharine Lee Bates taken from the college paper. O Love That Wilt Not Let Me Go was just getting under way, having emerged from a questionable 6/4 tune rhythm

into St. Margaret. His featuring of How Firm
a Foundation in its original form, spelling and all,
and the strength of Greek negatives makes the
last stanza take on new meaning: "I'll never, no
never, no never forsake." His one stanza inclusion
of Carlyle's translation of Ein Feste Burg Ist Unser
Gott, sung by all English-speaking peoples *except*
Americans, is timely. His discernment that Shepherd of Tender Youth is not an accurate translation
from the Greek but a spirited one; his quasi-refusal
to credit St. Bernard of Clairvaux as the author of
"Jesus, the very thought of thee"; his plea that
"Stand up, stand up for Jesus" is strengthened by
singing the original: "Each piece put on with
prayer" rather than the revised: "And watching
unto prayer" all testify to his scholarship and good
common sense. Again and again he uses the original text, including omitted and forgotten stanzas, to
reveal total lyric and devotional content. For other
hymns the revised and shortened forms prevail.

Of the one hundred and twenty hymns and their
stories in this volume, two thirds are still in use in
our latest and standard hymn books. These are
easy and delightful pages to read; try it and dis-
cover type measures $3\frac{1}{2}$ by $5\frac{1}{2}$ inches, a guarantee of
keen and continuing eyesight.

H. AUGUSTINE SMITH.

Boston University.

Contents

Contents

"All Hail the Power of Jesus' Name"
Edward Perronet

THIS, one of the greatest of hymns, was written by Edward Perronet, and is the one thing that has kept his name green in the earth.

Nevertheless, Perronet was a man worth knowing about, quite apart from his magnificent hymn. He was descended from French Protestants, and his father was an English clergyman who joined the Wesleys in carrying on their great revival of religion.

His son Edward also became a clergyman, and for a time labored with the Wesleys. Charles Wesley writes of his boldness in preaching. At one time he and Perronet were beset in a house by a mob of rough revilers, whom Perronet opposed courageously, while they abused him and threw dirt on him.

In his note-book, three years later, Charles Wesley speaks of a journey he made to London, with his brother John and with Perronet. "We were in perils of robbers, who were abroad, and had robbed many the night before," writes Wesley. But, he stoutly adds, "We commended ourselves to God, and rode over the heath singing." What a scene that must have been!

John Wesley wanted to hear Perronet preach, and Perronet, for some reason, would not preach before

Wesley. One day Wesley, seeing Perronet in the congregation, announced that he would preach the next morning. Perronet did not want to make a scene, so the next morning he mounted the pulpit, explained that he had not consented to preach and felt that he could not, but nevertheless he would give them the best sermon that had ever been delivered. Thereupon he opened the Bible, and read the Sermon on the Mount from beginning to end, and without a word of comment. A song and prayer finished the service.

After eight years of co-operation with the Wesleys, Perronet left them, disagreeing with some of their regulations. They continued, however, to esteem and love each other.

The last years of Perronet were spent at Canterbury, where he was pastor of an independent church, and where he died in 1792, at the age of sixty-six.

He published three volumes of religious poems, one being made up of versified Scripture. Some of these poems deserve to be widely used, as, for instance, the hymn containing the stanza :—

> " O grant me, Lord, that sweet content
>   That sweetens every state ;
>   Which no internal fears can rent,
>   Nor outward foes abate.''

None of Perronet's poems, however, have attained fame except the immortal "All hail the power of Jesus' name." It was written in 1779, and was first printed, in 1780, in *The Gospel Magazine*. The poet gave it the title, " On the Resurrection," and as he wrote it, there were eight stanzas, as follows :—

> All hail the power of Jesus' name,
>   Let angels prostrate fall ;
> Bring forth the royal diadem,
>   To crown Him Lord of all !
>
> Let high born seraphs tune the lyre,
>   And, as they tune it, fall
> Before His face who tunes their choir,
>   And crown Him Lord of all !
>
> Crown Him, ye morning stars of light,
>   Who fixed this floating ball,
> Now hail the Strength of Israel's might,
>   And crown Him Lord of all !
>
> Crown Him, ye martyrs of your God,
>   Who from His altar call ;
> Extol the stem of Jesse's rod,
>   And crown Him Lord of all !
>
> Ye seed of Israel's chosen race,
>   Ye ransomed of the fall,
> Hail Him who saves you by His grace
>   And crown Him Lord of all !
>
> Hail Him, ye heirs of David's line,
>   Whom David Lord did call,
> The God incarnate, Man divine,
>   And crown Him Lord of all !
>
> Sinners, whose love can ne'er forget
>   The wormwood and the gall,
> Go spread your trophies at His feet,
>   And crown Him Lord of all !

> Let every tribe and every tongue
> That bound creation's call
> Now shout in universal song,
> The crowned Lord of all !

As it now stands in our hymn-books, the hymn is shortened and changed, and one stanza has been added :—

> " Oh, that with yonder sacred throng
> We at His feet may fall ;
> We'll join the everlasting song,
> And crown Him Lord of all."

This last stanza was added by the famous hymn collector, Rev. John Rippon, in 1787.

At first the hymn was sung to the tune of "Miles' Lane," written for the hymn by William Shrubsole, a London organist, in 1780. Now, however, we use the tune "Coronation," which was composed in 1792, the year Perronet died, by Oliver Holden, a carpenter of Charlestown, Mass. Holden's queer old organ, on which this glorious tune was first played, is still to be seen in Boston.

The most famous story connected with Perronet's great hymn is told of the missionary to India, Rev. E. P. Scott. One day he saw on the street a man of so strange an appearance that he inquired about him, and learned that he belonged to a wild mountain tribe among whom Christ had never been preached. Mr. Scott prayed over the matter, and decided to visit that tribe.

As soon as he reached their mountain home, he fell in with a savage band who were on a war expedition.   They seized him, and pointed their spears at his heart.

At once the missionary drew out the violin that he always carried with him, and began to play and sing in the native language, "All hail the power of Jesus' name!"   He closed his eyes, expecting death at any minute.   When he reached the third stanza, as nothing had happened, he opened his eyes, and was amazed to see that the spears had fallen from the hands of the savages, and big tears were in their eyes!

They invited Mr. Scott to their homes, and he spent two and a half years among them, winning many of them to Christ.   When poor health compelled him to return to America, they followed him for thirty or forty miles, begging him to come back again.   This he did, and continued to work among them until his death.

"A Mighty Fortress is Our God"
Martin Luther

MARTIN LUTHER was born in Eisleben, Germany, in 1483, a poor miner's son.   His heart was full of music when he was a boy, and he used to sing from door to door.   After he became a man, and had led in the great revolt from the superstitions, sins, and injustices of the Roman Catholic Church, he did two things that more than all others established Protestantism firmly,—he translated the Bible into the language of the common people, and he wrote hymns also in their every-day language, to be sung to attractive, familiar tunes.

The first printed hymn-book was published at Wittenberg in 1524,—eight hymns with tunes, and four of them by Luther.   Since that beginning it is said that Germans have written more than 100,000 hymns, and the greatest of all is this hymn of Luther's. Luther wrote some thirty-six hymns in all, but this is his noblest.   Some say that the strong tune to which the hymn is always sung was composed by Luther, but he probably merely adapted a tune already in existence.

The hymn was written about 1528, and though many attempts have been made to associate it with various stirring events in the life of the great reformer, it is not known what occasion prompted it.

He based it on the Forty-sixth Psalm, but it does not follow the course of the psalm ; it merely catches up and carries on the psalm's leading thought.

Whatever its origin, "Ein' Feste Burg ist Unser Gott" had an immediate influence in Germany, and became for the Reformation what the great French hymn, La Marseillaise, became to France.   It is now the national hymn of the Fatherland.

Says Dr. Benson :

"It was sung at Augsburg during the Diet, and in all the churches of Saxony, often against the protest of the priest.   It was sung in the streets ; and, so heard, comforted the hearts of Melanchthon, Jonas, and Cruciger, as they entered Weimar, when banished from Wittenberg in 1547.

"It was sung by poor Protestant emigrants on their way into exile, and by martyrs at their death. It is woven into the web of history of Reformation times, and it became the true national hymn of Protestant Germany.

"Gustavus Adolphus ordered it sung by his army before the battle of Leipzig, in 1631, and on the field of that battle it was repeated, more than two centuries afterward, by the throng assembled at the jubilee of the Gustavus Adolphus Association.   Again it was the battle hymn of his army at Lützen, in 1632, in which the king was slain, but his army won the victory.

"It has had a part in countless celebrations commemorating the men and events of the Reformation ; and its first line is engraved on the base of Luther's monument at Wittenberg."

Luther comforted his own heart with the hymn, and when his great cause seemed almost lost he would turn to his friend Melanchthon and say, "Come, Philip, let us sing the Forty-sixth Psalm."

There is a story of the use of it by the German troops lodged in a church after the battle of Sedan. They were too excited to sleep. At last some one began to play Luther's hymn upon the organ. The soldiers united in a splendid outburst of song, after which they fell into peaceful slumber.

The hymn has been translated into English more than eighty times, but only twice with such success that the result has won popular favor. In England, they sing the translation made by Thomas Carlyle, who was the one that introduced the hymn in that land, in 1831. His first stanza is:

> A sure stronghold our God is He,
>   A trusty shield and weapon;
> Our help He'll be, and set us free
>   From every ill can happen.
> That old malicious foe
> Intends us deadly woe;
> Armèd with might from hell
> And deepest craft as well,
>   On earth is not his fellow.

Our favorite American version is that by Rev. Frederic Henry Hedge, a great German scholar, himself a poet of no mean ability, whose translation appeared in 1852. Longfellow has a version in his "Golden Legend," and one of Whittier's war poems is in Luther's metre, and is called, "Ein' Feste Burg ist Unser Gott." Here is Dr. Hedge's translation:

A mighty Fortress is our God,
A Bulwark never failing;
Our Helper He amid the flood
Of mortal ills prevailing:
For still our ancient foe
Doth seek to work us woe;
His craft and power are great,
And, armed with cruel hate,
On earth is not his equal.

Did we in our own strength confide,
Our striving would be losing;
Were not the right man on our side,
The man of God's own choosing:
Dost ask who that may be?
Christ Jesus, it is He;
Lord Sabaoth His name,
From age to age the same,
And He must win the battle.

And though this world, with devils filled,
Should threaten to undo us;
We will not fear, for God hath willed
His truth to triumph through us.
The prince of darkness grim,—
We tremble not for him;
His rage we can endure,
For lo! his doom is sure,
One little word shall fell him.

That word above all earthly powers,
No thanks to them, abideth;
The Spirit and the gifts are ours
Through Him who with us sideth:
Let goods and kindred go,
This mortal life also;
The body they may kill:
God's truth abideth still,
His kingdom is for ever.

"Calm on the Listening Ear of Night"
Edmund Hamilton Sears

TO be the author of two of the most famous and helpful of Christmas hymns is glory enough for any man. That was the blessed result of the life of Rev. Edmund Hamilton Sears, D. D. He was a busy pastor; he wrote four or five books and many other poems, but long after all his other work is forgotten those two Christmas hymns will be remembered and sung.

Dr. Sears was born, lived, and died in a narrow region in Massachusetts. His birth was in 1810, at Sandisfield, and his death was on January 14, 1876, at Weston. He was a Swedenborgian in belief, but he was the pastor of Unitarian churches.

When he was a young man, in 1834, Mr. Sears wrote the first of his two splendid Christmas odes; when he was in the prime of life, in 1850, he wrote the second, "It came upon the midnight clear." It is the first that is here given, the lovely Advent poem, "Calm on the listening ear of night." The two hymns are alike and yet different. In Dr. Sears's volume, "Sermons and Songs," they stand, the one preceding and the other following a sermon for Christmas Eve on 1 Tim. 2:6. And here is our hymn, just as it appears in that book :—

Calm on the listening ear of night
  Come heaven's melodious strains,
Where wild Judæa stretches forth
  Her silver mantled plains ;
Celestial choirs from courts above
  Shed sacred glories there,
And angels, with their sparkling lyres,
  Make music on the air.

The answering hills of Palestine
  Send back the glad reply,
And greet from all their holy heights
  The Day-Spring from on high ;
O'er the blue depths of Galilee,
  There comes a holier calm,
And Sharon waves, in solemn praise,
  Her silent groves of palm.

" Glory to God ! "   The lofty strain
  The realm of ether fills ;
How sweeps the song of solemn joy
  O'er Judah's sacred hills !
" Glory to God ! "   The sounding skies
  Loud with their anthems ring,
" Peace on the earth ; good will to men
  From heaven's Eternal King."

Light on thy hills, Jerusalem !
  The Saviour now is born,
And bright on Bethlehem's joyous plains
  Breaks the first Christmas morn,
And brightly on Moriah's brow
  Crowned with her temple spires,
Which first proclaim the new-born light,
  Clothed with its orient fires.

This day shall Christian tongues be mute,
    And Christian hearts be cold?
Oh, catch the anthem that from heaven
    O'er Judah's mountains rolled,
When burst upon that listening night
    The high and solemn lay :
" Glory to God, on earth be peace,"
    Salvation comes to-day !

" O Little Town of Bethlehem "
Bishop Brooks

WHEN Phillips Brooks, the beloved and great preacher, was a boy, his parents had him and his brothers learn hymns. They used to enjoy reciting them on Sunday evenings, and when Phillips went to college he could repeat some two hundred of them. He never forgot them, and they often came up in his wonderful sermons.

It is not at all surprising, then, that Phillips Brooks began to write hymns himself. He often composed poems, and some of his poems have become very dear to all Christians. One of the best of these is the beautiful Christmas hymn that we have chosen for our study.

It is not at all surprising, either, that the great preacher should write poems for children. He loved all children, and liked nothing better, giant of a man as he was, than to get down on the floor and romp with them. He often wrote letters to his child friends, and these letters are among the most delightful bits of his writing.

Mr. Brooks preached in Philadelphia first, and then in Boston. Our hymn was written when he was rector of the Holy Trinity Church of Philadelphia, and for his Sunday-school. It was used by

the children at their Christmas service in the year
1868.   How little they understood what a famous
song they were singing for the first time!

The lovely tune, "St. Louis," to which the hymn
is usually sung, was written for it at that time by
Mr. Lewis H. Redner, the organist of the church,
the superintendent of the Sunday-school, and teacher
of one of the classes.   It was in the middle of the
night before that Christmas service that Mr. Redner
woke up suddenly with angelic strains ringing in his
ears.   He took a piece of music-paper and jotted
down the melody of the tune; then the next morning, before going to church, he filled in the harmony.
So little did he, too, understand what a great thing
he was doing.

It was a long time before the churches realized the
beauty of the song.   Not until 1892 was the hymn
admitted to the hymnal of Bishop Brooks's own
denomination.

Here is the Christmas carol, as Phillips Brooks
wrote it.   The fourth stanza is unfamiliar, because
the writer himself left it out of the later copies of the
poem; but you will want to see it.

O little town of Bethlehem,
  How still we see thee lie!
Above thy deep and dreamless sleep
  The silent stars go by:
Yet in thy dark streets shineth
  The everlasting Light;
The hopes and fears of all the years
  Are met in thee to-night.

For Christ is born of Mary;
  And gathered all above,
While mortals sleep, the angels keep
  Their watch of wondering love.
O morning stars together
  Proclaim the holy birth;
And praises sing to God the King,
  And peace to men on earth.

How silently, how silently,
  The wondrous Gift is given!
So God imparts to human hearts
  The blessings of His heaven.
No ear may hear His coming,
  But in this world of sin,
Where meek souls will receive Him still,
  The dear Christ enters in.

Where children pure and happy
  Pray to the blessed Child,
Where misery cries out to Thee,
  Son of the Mother mild;
Where Charity stands watching,
  And Faith holds wide the Door,
The dark night wakes, the glory breaks,
  And Christmas comes once more.

O holy Child of Bethlehem,
  Descend to us, we pray;
Cast out our sin, and enter in,
  Be born in us to-day.
We hear the Christmas angels
  The great glad tidings tell;
O come to us, abide with us,
  Our Lord Emmanuel.

"From Greenland's Icy Mountains"
Bishop Heber

ONE of the greatest and noblest of all hymn-writers is Reginald Heber. He was born April 21, 1783, at Malpas, Cheshire, England. His father gave him every advantage, and he made the best use of his opportunities. He became a distinguished poet when a young man at Oxford. The first year after entering, when only seventeen years old, he took a prize for a Latin poem, and two years afterward he won a prize by a remarkable poem on Palestine, which was received with such applause as had never before been heard in that sedate gathering. After this success his parents found him on his knees in grateful prayer.

He became a minister of the Church of England, and began to write hymns. It was just becoming the custom to use hymns in Episcopal churches, and there were no hymn-books.

The Christians of England were aroused at that time to the great call of foreign missions, and a collection was ordered to be taken for that object in all the churches.

On Saturday, May 29, 1819, young Heber happened to be visiting his father-in-law, in whose church he was to preach the next day. This collection was to be taken, and a suitable hymn was wanted. They asked Heber to write one.

He retired to another part of the room, and in a short time read the first three stanzas of his famous hymn.

"There ! That will do very well," they told him.

"No, no, the sense is not complete," answered Heber ; so he added the splendid fourth stanza, the entire hymn being as follows, according to the poet's own manuscript, which has fortunately been preserved for us (bringing $210 when sold,—a sum larger than the missionary collection received when it was first sung) :—

From Greenland's icy mountains,
  From India's coral strand,
Where Afric's sunny fountains
  Roll down their golden strand,
From many an ancient river,
  From many a palmy plain,
They call us to deliver
  Their land from error's chain.

What though the spicy breezes
  Blow soft o'er Ceylon's isle ;
Though every prospect pleases,
  And only man is vile :
In vain with lavish kindness
  The gifts of God are strown ;
The heathen in his blindness
  Bows down to wood and stone.

Can we, whose souls are lighted
  With wisdom from on high,
Can we to men benighted
  The lamp of life deny ?

Salvation !   O salvation !
    The joyful sound proclaim,
Till each remotest nation
    Has learned Messiah's Name.

Waft, waft, ye winds, His story,
    And you, ye waters, roll,
Till like a sea of glory
    It spreads from pole to pole ;
Till o'er our ransomed nature
    The Lamb for sinners slain,
Redeemer, King, Creator,
    In bliss returns to reign.

The beautiful and stirring tune to which the hymn is always sung was written as rapidly as the hymn itself.

A printed copy of the poem reached Miss Mary W. Howard, of Savannah, Ga.   She admired it greatly, and wanted a tune for it.   The metre was a new one at that time.   So Miss Howard sent the poem to Lowell Mason, then a young bank clerk and singing-teacher in Savannah.   In half an hour he sent back the "Missionary Hymn" tune that is universally used.

When Heber was forty years old, he became first bishop of Calcutta.   He refused the appointment twice, for he dearly loved his quiet home and church, but his sense of duty finally compelled him to accept.   As he went out to the India of which he had sung, he had an opportunity to breathe the "spicy breezes" that "blow soft o'er Ceylon's isle," and that carry the fragrance of the aromatic forests far out to sea.

His duties and authority extended all over India, Ceylon, Mauritius, and Australasia. He entered upon his work with great energy. It was he who ordained the first native minister, Christian David. He traveled far and wide, but the climate and the heavy tasks quite wore him out. In less than three years, on April 3, 1826, the good bishop suddenly died.

Heber was greatly beloved. Thackeray called him " one of the best of English gentlemen." He wrote fifty-seven hymns, which were published after his death in one book. It is said that every one of these hymns is in use—an honor paid to no other hymn-writer that ever lived.

His missionary hymn is his most famous production, and some one has ventured to say that it has accomplished as much for foreign missions as all the missionary sermons ever preached,—a statement he would be the first to rebuke.

But Heber wrote other great hymns, the greatest being the noblest hymn of adoration in the language, " Holy, holy, holy, Lord God Almighty ! " Tennyson pronounced this the finest hymn ever written in any language.

He also wrote the noblest warrior hymn ever composed: " The Son of God goes forth to war." Another favorite is his " Brightest and best of the sons of the morning." Still others are: " By cool Siloam's shady rill," " Lord of mercy and of might," and " Bread of the world in mercy broken."

Altogether, though not the greatest of English

hymn-writers, Heber may fairly be called the most
poetical of them all ; and his beautiful personal character, when one knows about it, adds a new beauty
to his lovely hymns.

"Speed Away!"
Fanny Crosby

FANNY CROSBY is one of the greatest of the world's hymn-writers; perhaps only Watts and Wesley would rank above her. She is great in the number of her hymns—more than three thousand, and in the large number of them that have found favor with Christians and seem destined to live forever. To name only a few, what immortal glory belongs to the author of "Pass me not, O gentle Saviour," "Rescue the perishing," "I am Thine, O Lord," "Blessed assurance, Jesus is mine," "Jesus, keep me near the cross," "'Tis the blessed hour of prayer," "Safe in the arms of Jesus," "Some day the silver cord will break," "Thou, my everlasting portion," "Saviour, more than life to me," "All the way my Saviour leads me," "Hide Thou me," "Jesus is tenderly calling thee home," "Lord, at Thy mercy-seat humbly I fall," and many other hymns almost as well known.

Frances Jane Crosby was born in Southeast, N. Y., on March 24, 1820. She is ninety-four years old as this book is published, but is still, I believe, in excellent health.

She has been blind since she was six months old, but she is of a happy, contented disposition, and

refuses to be pitied because of her great affliction.
Indeed, when only eight years old she wrote :—

" O what a happy soul am I !
Although I cannot see,
I am resolved that in this world
Contented I will be ;
How many blessings I enjoy
That other people don't !
To weep and sigh because I'm blind,
I cannot, and I won't."

Fanny Crosby spent twelve years as a pupil in the
New York Institution for the blind, and there she was
a teacher from 1847 to 1858, teaching language and
history.   While she was yet a pupil she was a splendid illustration of what education can do for the
blind, and once she recited a poem on the subject
before the Senate and House of Representatives at
Washington, and also before the governor and legislature of New Jersey.

In 1845 she began to write words for the music of
George F. Root, who became music-teacher in the
institution.   Many of these songs became famous,
and the royalties on one of them, " Rosalie, the
Prairie Flower," amounted to nearly three thousand dollars.   Another well-known song of hers is
"There's music in the air."

It was not, however, till February 5, 1864, that she
wrote her first hymn.   It was written for W. B. Brad-
bury, and ever since that time he, and his successors,
Biglow and Main, have been her publishers, accept-
ing and paying for all that she writes.   She has

written many hymns for such singers and composers as Sankey, Doane, Lowry, Philip Phillips, Sweney, Sherwin and Kirkpatrick. Her songs have blessed thousands of lives, and there is scarcely one of them but has won many souls to the Saviour.

In 1858 Miss Crosby was married to another pupil of the institution, Alexander Van Alstyne, a musician. She sometimes uses her full name, but often signs her hymns with pen names: A., C., D. H. W., V. A., Ella Dale; Jenny V., Mrs. Jenie Glenn, Mrs. Kate Grinley, Viola, Grace J. Francis, Mrs. C. M. Wilson, Lizzie Edwards, Henrietta E. Blair, Rose Atherton, Maud Marion, Leah Carlton, and still others!

She writes very rapidly, and some of her most famous hymns have been dictated almost as fast as the words could be taken down. Her hymns are full of the Bible with which her memory is stored. When she was a mere child she committed to memory the first four books of the Old Testament and the four Gospels.

In her home at Bridgeport, Conn., the aged singer sits peacefully awaiting the call to the world where she shall see all beautiful things and shall join—and what voice will be sweeter?—in the song of Moses and the Lamb.

The hymn by her which we have chosen as characteristic is "Speed away"—a song that has done much to arouse interest in missions. It has become the missionary farewell hymn, being sung at the parting with hundreds of missionaries as they set out upon their noble errands.

Speed away! speed away on your mission of light,
To the lands that are lying in darkness and night;
'Tis the Master's command; go ye forth in His name,
The wonderful gospel of Jesus proclaim;
Take your lives in your hand, to the work while 'tis day,
Speed away! speed away! speed away!

Speed away, speed away with the life-giving Word,
To the nations that know not the voice of the Lord;
Take the wings of the morning and fly o'er the wave,
In the strength of your Master the lost ones to save;
He is calling once more, not a moment's delay,
Speed away! speed away! speed away!

Speed away, speed away with the message of rest,
To the souls by the tempter in bondage oppressed;
For the Saviour has purchased their ransom from sin,
And the banquet is ready.   O gather them in;
To the rescue make haste, there's no time for delay,
Speed away! speed away! speed away!

"How Firm a Foundation"
Probably by Robert Keene

OUR modern hymn-books give but six of the seven original stanzas of the hymn, "How firm a foundation." We give here the entire hymn. It first appeared in a book entitled "A Selection of Hymns from the Best Authors," published in 1787 by a Baptist minister of London, Dr. John Rippon, who, though an ardent admirer of Watts, desired to have some hymns in addition to those by the great hymn-writer. Many of the hymns in his collection were there gathered for the first time, and have been in use ever since. We print the hymn precisely as it stood in Dr. Rippon's book, old style s's and all:

SCRIPTURE PROMISES

CXXVIII. Elevens. K——

Exceeding great and precious Promiſes, 2 Pet. iii. 4

1 How firm a Foundation, ye Saints of the Lord,
  Is laid for your Faith in his excellent Word ;
  What more can he ſay than to you he hath ſaid ?
  You, who unto Jesus for Refuge have fled.

2 In every Condition, in Sickneſs, in Health,
  In Poverty's Vale, or abounding in Wealth ;
  At Home and Abroad, on the Land, on the Sea,
  " As thy Days may demand, ſhall thy Strength ever be.

3 " Fear not, I am with thee, O be not difmay'd,
  " I, I am thy God, and will ftill give thee Aid ;
  " I'll ftrengthen thee, help thee, and caufe thee to ftand,
  " Upheld by my righteous omnipotent Hand.

4 " When thro' the deep Waters I call thee to go,
  " The Rivers of Woe fhall not thee overflow ;
  " For I will be with thee, thy Troubles to blefs,
  " And fanctify to thee, thy deepeft Diftrefs.

5 " When thro' fiery Trials thy Pathway fhall lie,
  " My Grace all fufficient fhall be thy Supply ;
  " The Flame fhall not hurt thee, I only defign
  " Thy Drofs to confume, and thy Gold to refine.

6 " Even down to old Age, all my People fhall prove
  " My fovereign, eternal, unchangeable Love ;
  " And when hoary Hairs fhall their Temples adorn,
  " Like lambs they fhall ftill in my bofom be borne.

7 " The Soul that on JESUS hath lean'd for Repofe,
  " *I will not, I will not* defert to his Foes ;
  " That Soul, tho' all Hell fhould endeavor to fhake,
  " *I'll never—no never*—no never forfake." [1]

[1] Agreeable to Dr. Doddridge's Tranflation of Heb. xiii. 5.

Notice the " K——" following the " Elevens," which indicates the number of syllables. That K—— is all that is positively known about the author. After Dr. Rippon's death some one changed the " K——" in later editions to " Kirkham," but it is not thought that Thomas Kirkham wrote it. Daniel Sedgwick, an old-time student of hymns, heard an old lady in an almshouse say that the hymn was written by George Keith, a hymn-writer of the day, and on that slender ground most of our modern hymnals attribute it to him. It is quite certain, however, that the author was Robert Keene, who was precentor in Dr. Rippon's church, and who also wrote the tune "Geard," to which it was originally sung.

We sing the hymn to the tune called "Portuguese Hymn," because some one heard it in the chapel of the Portuguese Embassy in London, and jumped to the conclusion that it was Portuguese in its origin. It is not, however, but is the music of a Latin Christmas hymn, "Adeste Fideles"—the hymn which we have translated in the familiar "O come, all ye faithful." "John Reading" is falsely given by many books as the composer of this tune.

General Curtis Guild, Jr., has told in *The Sunday School Times* how this hymn, "How firm a foundation," thus wedded to a Christmas tune, was sung on a famous Christmas morning. The Seventh Army Corps was encamped on the hills above Havana, Cuba, on Christmas Eve of 1898—a beautiful tropical night. Suddenly a sentinel from the camp of the Forty-ninth Iowa called, "Number ten ; twelve o'clock, and all's well !" A strong voice raised the chorus, and many manly voices joined in until the whole regiment was singing. Then the Sixth Missouri added its voices, and the Fourth Virginia, and all the rest, till there, as General Guild said, " on the long ridges above the great city whence Spanish tyranny once went forth to enslave the New World, a whole American army corps was singing :

" 'Fear not, I am with thee, O be not dismayed ;
    I, I am thy God, and will still give thee aid ;
    I'll strengthen thee, help thee, and cause thee to stand,
    Upheld by my righteous, omnipotent hand.'

"The Northern soldier knew the hymn as one he
had learned beside his mother's knee. To the
Southern soldier it was that and something more ;
it was the favorite hymn of General Robert E. Lee,
and was sung at that great commander's funeral.

" Protestant and Catholic, South and North, singing together on Christmas day in the morning—
that's an American army ! "

Notice the Scripture reference that follows the
title, " Exceeding great and precious Promifes."
Look it up, and note its appropriateness.

Notice also the second stanza, omitted from many
modern hymnals. Would you willingly lose it?
When it is omitted, the real beginning of the Scripture quotation which answers the question, "What
more can He say ? " is left out. After the first seven
lines, the rest of the hymn is all Bible.

Notice, too, the last line, with its footnote referring
to Doddridge's translation of Heb. 13 : 5. This
translation brings out more clearly than our Revised
or Authorized versions the multiplied negatives of
the original Greek : " I will not, I will not leave thee,
I will never, never, never forsake thee."

The story is told of the venerable Dr. Charles
Hodge, so greatly honored and beloved at Princeton,
that one evening, when conducting prayers, the old
man was reading this hymn, but was so overcome

by its exalted sentiments, especially in view of his own close approach to the better land, that he had no voice for the last line, but could only indicate it by gestures, beating out the rhythm of the words.

Andrew Jackson, after retiring from the Presidency, became a devout member of the Presbyterian church. One day in his old age a company of visitors was with him, when General Jackson said, "There is a beautiful hymn on the subject of the exceeding great and precious promises of God to His people. It was a favorite hymn with my dear wife till the day of her death. It begins thus : ' How firm a foundation, ye saints of the Lord.' I wish you would sing it now." So the company did what was asked by the old hero.

Miss Willard wrote once: "Mother says that at family prayers in her home they were wont to sing together, ' How firm a foundation ' ; and her parents used to say it would never wear out, because it was so full of Scripture. When mother came back to us after being confined to her room six weeks, we sang that hymn for her, and she broke in at the verse about ' hoary hairs ' and said : ' How I enjoyed that for my old grandmother who lived to be ninety-seven, and I enjoyed it for my dear father who was eighty-six when he passed away ; and now my daughter enjoys it for me, who am eighty-four, and perhaps she will live on to be as old as I, when I feel sure she will have friends who will enjoy it just as tenderly for her.' "

A beautiful story is told of that noble woman, Fidelia Fisk, the devoted missionary to the women of

Persia. One time when she was worn out with her
heavy and difficult labors, she was attending a meeting. Her weary body greatly needed rest. Of a
sudden a native woman came behind her as she sat
on a mat, and whispered, "Lean on me." Miss
Fisk heard, but scarcely heeded. Then again came
the whisper, "Lean on me." Miss Fisk then leaned
gently on her unknown friend. But again came the
whisper, "If you love me, lean hard." The worn-
out missionary took the words as a message from
her Father in heaven, urging her, if she loved Him,
to lean hard upon Him.

At one time a pastor told this touching story to
his people in a Kansas village. They were greatly
discouraged because of the failure of their crops.
As soon as the story was finished, the minister sat
down and let the people make their own application.
At once a voice struck up our hymn, and one after
another joined in until the little company had begun
once more to "lean for repose" on the never-failing
Arms :

> " The soul that on Jesus hath leaned for repose
> I will not, I will not desert to its foes ;
> That soul, though all hell should endeavor to shake,
> I'll never, no never, no never forsake."

"My Country, 'Tis of Thee"

Samuel Francis Smith

OLIVER WENDELL HOLMES wrote many poems for the reunions of his class at Harvard, the famous class of 1829, and one of them, written when all the class were gray-heads, contains these lines :—

> " And there's a nice youngster of excellent pith,—
> Fate tried to conceal him by naming him Smith ;
> But he shouted a song for the brave and the free,—
> Just read on his medal, ' My country,' ' of thee.' "

This "Smith" was Samuel Francis Smith, who wrote our American national anthem. He was born in Boston, October 21, 1808 ; graduated from Harvard, and studied for the ministry at Andover, becoming a Baptist clergyman.

It was while he was at Andover that he wrote the famous hymn. Lowell Mason, the eminent composer, had given him some collections of German songs for children, that he might translate them into English. "One dismal day in February, 1832," Dr. Smith wrote long afterward, "about half an hour before sunset, I was turning over the leaves of one of the music books, when my eye rested on the tune which is now known as ' America.' I liked the spirited movement of it, not knowing it at that time to be 'God Save the King.'   I glanced at the German words and saw that they were patriotic, and instantly felt the impulse to write a patriotic hymn of my own, adapted to the tune.   Picking up a scrap of waste paper which lay near me, I wrote at once, probably within half an hour, the hymn 'America,' as it is now known everywhere.   The whole hymn stands to-day as it stood on the bit of waste paper, five or six inches long and two and a half wide."

This is the hymn :—

My country, 'tis of thee,
Sweet land of liberty,
      Of thee I sing ;
Land where my fathers died,
Land of the pilgrims' pride,
From every mountain side
      Let freedom ring.

My native country,—thee,
Land of the noble free,—
      Thy name I love ;
I love thy rocks and rills,
Thy woods and templed hills ;
My heart with rapture thrills
      Like that above.

Let music swell the breeze,
And ring from all the trees
      Sweet freedom's song :
Let mortal tongues awake ;
Let all that breathe partake ;
Let rocks their silence break,
      The sound prolong.

Our fathers' God, to Thee,
Author of liberty,
    To Thee we sing;
Long may our land be bright
With freedom's holy light;
Protect us by Thy might,
    Great God, our King.

"I never designed it for a national hymn," Dr.
Smith said afterward; "I never supposed I was
writing one." Many of the best things come in just
that unconscious way.

On the Fourth of July of that same year, 1832, the
hymn was first sung, under Mr. Mason's superin-
tendency, at a children's celebration in Park Street
Church, Boston, and soon the song of the young
poet became popular everywhere. It has never been
adopted by our government as a national anthem,
but it has been adopted by the people themselves,
which is far better.

Dr. Smith became an honored pastor, in several
important churches. At one time he was a professor
of modern languages, for he was familiar with fifteen
languages, and some one who visited him in his
eighty-sixth year found the vigorous old man looking around for a text-book with which to begin the
study of Russian!

At one time he was editor of *The Baptist Missionary Magazine;* at another time of *The Christian Review.* For fifteen years he was secretary of the
American Baptist Missionary Union. He was deeply
interested in missions, and only second in fame to his
national anthem is his missionary hymn, "The morn-

ing light is breaking." It was he who did much toward saving the " Lone Star " mission in India, by writing his poem with that title. Other well-known hymns of his are " To-day the Saviour calls " and " Softly fades the twilight ray."

The fact that " My country, 'tis of thee " is written to the same tune as the English national anthem, " God save the King," has given rise to many stirring scenes at Christian Endeavor conventions all over the world. Very often one stanza of each anthem is sung, the conclusion being one stanza of " Blest be the tie."

This was done at the magnificent meeting on Boston Common, at the Christian Endeavor Convention of July, 1895. Eleven thousand persons were present in the great tent, and Dr. Smith probably never received such an ovation as when he came forward to read the poem which he wrote for the occasion, " Arouse ye, arouse ye, O servants of God." The noble verses were read with much fervor, though in a voice whose strength had been stolen by many years.

On November 19 of that same year the aged poet passed away. He died in the harness, just as he was taking the train to preach in a neighboring town on the following Sunday. And so passed from earth the Christian patriot, whose love for his country widened out into the missionary love for all the world.

"God Bless Our Native Land"

Charles T. Brooks and John S. Dwight

THIS brief hymn of only two stanzas is one of the best patriotic hymns ever written. Strangely enough, it is uncertain just who wrote it, and when it was composed. At least four different writers have declared positively that the hymn was their own.

It is certain, however, that the poem was written jointly by two Unitarian clergymen, life-long friends, —Rev. Charles Timothy Brooks and Dr. John Sullivan Dwight. These were both Massachusetts men, the first being born in Salem, and the second in Boston. They were born the same year, 1813, and graduated from Harvard the same year, 1832. Their deaths occurred in each case at an advanced age, but there was here a separation of ten years, for Mr. Brooks passed away in 1883, and Dr. Dwight in 1893.

Both were men of gentle and retiring disposition. Mr. Brooks was active in literary work, especially as a translator. Dr. Dwight was for many years a leader in the musical interests of Boston, and founded in 1852 *Dwight's Journal of Music*, which he continued until 1881. Dr. Dwight was one of the band of enthusiasts who joined in the famous experiment of Brook Farm, where a company of lofty thinkers endeavored to put into practice their theories of simple, ideal living.

47

Both Mr. Brooks and Dr. Dwight laid claim at different times to be the author of this hymn, but the truth seems to be that each had a hand in the matter, and it is possible that it was translated from the German, or, at least, that a German poem furnished the fundamental idea. At any rate, the hymn first appeared in Lowell Mason's *Carmina Sacra*, in 1841.

The following is the form in which it was there printed. Although there are several versions, this is the best:

God bless our native land ;
Firm may she ever stand
    Through storm and night :
When the wild tempests rave,
Ruler of wind and wave,
Do Thou our country save
    By Thy great might.

For her our prayers shall rise
To God, above the skies ;
    On Him we wait ;
Thou who art ever nigh,
Guarding with watchful eye,
To Thee aloud we cry,
    God save the state.

"Jesus, Lover of My Soul"
Charles Wesley

THE three greatest hymn-writers of our English tongue are Isaac Watts, Charles Wesley, and Fanny Crosby. There are many who think that the hymn we are to study is the greatest hymn ever written; all men agree that it is the best of Wesley's hymns, though he wrote no less than six thousand. Many of these six thousand, too, rise to the highest rank of religious poetry, such as those beginning: "Ye servants of God, your Master proclaim," "Come, Thou long-expected Jesus," "A charge to keep I have," "Arise, my soul, arise," "Love divine, all love excelling," "Depth of mercy! Can there be," "Soldiers of Christ, arise," "Oh, for a thousand tongues to sing," and the noble Christmas hymn, "Hark! the herald angels sing." That is a wonderful list of great hymns to be written by one man.

Charles Wesley, next to the youngest of nineteen children, was born at Epworth, England, on December 18, 1708. His father was Rev. Samuel Wesley, and his mother, Susannah Wesley, was a very remarkable woman. When he was a lad of fifteen, an Irish member of Parliament, Garret Wesley, a wealthy man, wanted to adopt him. His father left him to decide the matter, and he decided in the negative. The boy that was finally adopted be-

49

came the father of the Duke of Wellington (Lord
"Wellesley," as he spelled "Wesley"), who conquered Napoleon at Waterloo.   How history might
have been changed if young Charles Wesley had
not decided as he did !

In 1735 Wesley became a clergyman of the Church
of England, and went with his brother John on a
missionary journey to Georgia, becoming secretary
to Governor Oglethorpe.   Within a year, broken in
health and discouraged, he was compelled to return
to England.

Years before this, when Charles Wesley was at
Oxford, he and his comrades were so strict in their
religious *methods* that they were nicknamed "Methodists."   But both Charles and John had to learn
more truly what religion really is.   Charles first
learned it from Peter Böhler, a Moravian of devout
spirit, and from Thomas Bray, an unlearned mechanic who knew Jesus Christ.   John soon after had
the same experience, and from their vivified preaching sprung the great Methodist churches of to-day.
Under the preaching of the Wesleys—especially that
of John Wesley, for Charles soon withdrew from the
more active work—revivals flamed all over England.
There was much persecution.   Charles himself was
driven from his church.   Many of his hymns were
written in time of trial, and it is said that "Jesus,
Lover of my soul," was written just after the poet
and his brother had been driven by a violent mob
from the place where they had been preaching.
Another story (and neither tale can be verified) says
that the hymn was written just after a frightened

little bird, pursued by a hawk, had flown into Wesley's window and crept into the folds of his coat. The
probable date of the hymn is 1740. After a long
life of nearly eighty years, Charles Wesley died,
March 29, 1788.

Here is his great hymn, including the third stanza,
which is now never sung :—

> Jesus, lover of my soul,
>   Let me to Thy bosom fly,
> While the nearer waters roll,
>   While the tempest still is high !
> Hide me, O my Saviour, hide,
>   Till the storm of life be past ;
> Safe into the haven guide,
>   Oh, receive my soul at last !

> Other refuge have I none,
>   Hangs my helpless soul on Thee ;
> Leave, ah ! leave me not alone,
>   Still support and comfort me !
> All my trust on Thee is stayed,
>   All my help from Thee I bring ;
> Cover my defenceless head
>   With the shadow of Thy wing.

> Wilt Thou not regard my call ?
>   Wilt Thou not accept my prayer ?
> Lo ! I sink, I faint, I fall —
>   Lo ! on Thee I cast my care :
> Reach me out Thy gracious hand !
>   While I of Thy strength receive,
> Hoping against hope I stand,
>   Dying, and, behold, I live !

Thou, O Christ, art all I want;
  More than all in Thee I find:
Raise the fallen, cheer the faint,
  Heal the sick, and lead the blind.
Just and holy is Thy name;
  I am all unrighteousness:
False and full of sin I am;
  Thou art full of truth and grace.

Plenteous grace with Thee is found,
  Grace to cover all my sin;
Let the healing streams abound,
  Make and keep me pure within.
Thou of life the fountain art;
  Freely let me take of Thee:
Spring Thou up within my heart,
  Rise to all eternity!

This was Finney's last song, sung by him the day before his death. The hymn has brought comfort to innumerable death-beds.

Just before the battle of Chickamauga a drummer-boy dreamed that he had gone home and was greeted by his dear mother and sister. He awoke very sad, because both mother and sister were dead, and he had no home. He told the little story to the chaplain before he went into the battle. He was left on the field with the dead and dying, and in the quiet of the night his voice was heard singing "Jesus, Lover of my soul." No one dared go to him. When he reached the lines,

"Leave, ah! leave me not alone,
  Still support and comfort me,"

his voice grew silent; and the next day his body was found leaning against a stump, beside his drum. He had indeed gone home to his mother and sister.

Another beautiful story is told of this hymn in connection with the Civil War. In a company of old soldiers, from the Union and Confederate armies, a former Confederate was telling how he had been detailed one night to shoot a certain exposed sentry of the opposing army. He had crept near and was about to fire with deadly aim when the sentry began to sing, "Jesus, Lover of my soul." He came to the words,

> "Cover my defenceless head
> With the shadow of Thy wing."

The hidden Confederate lowered his gun and stole away. "I can't kill that man," said he, "though he were ten times my enemy."

In the company was an old Union soldier who asked quickly,

"Was that in the Atlanta campaign of '64?"

"Yes."

"Then I was the Union sentry!"

And he went on to tell how, on that night, knowing the danger of his post, he had been greatly depressed, and, to keep up his courage, had begun to hum that hymn. By the time he had finished, he was entirely calm and fearless. Through the song God had spoken to two souls.

" Nearer, My God, to Thee "

Sarah Flower Adams

THIS is the greatest hymn ever written by a woman. Its author was the daughter of Benjamin Flower, an Englishman whose liberal views on politics caused his imprisonment in the Newgate Prison, London, for six months. While there, he was visited by Miss Eliza Gould, whose views were like his. After his release she married him, and they had two daughters, Eliza and Sarah.

It was Sarah who wrote the great hymn. She was born at Harlow, February 22, 1805. The mother died five years later of consumption, and both girls inherited her delicate constitution. Eliza was musical, and often wrote music for her sister's songs. Sarah, beautiful and vivacious, was fond of acting, and had an idea that the drama could be made to teach great truths as well as the pulpit. Fortunately, however, her frail body compelled her to give up the actor's career.

Miss Flower married, in 1834, a civil engineer, John Brydges Adams, and they made their home in London. Her beauty, her gay manners, her bright conversation, and her exalted character, made a deep impression upon many.

Eliza, the elder sister, became weakened in caring for Sarah through a long illness, and Sarah's death, in turn, was hastened, doubtless, by her care for Eliza in her last sickness. The two passed away within a short interval, the elder in December, 1846, and Sarah on August 14, 1848. The hymns sung at both funerals were by Sarah, with music by Eliza.

The great hymn was written in 1840, and was first published the following year in a book, "Hymns and Anthems," prepared by Mrs. Adams's pastor, Rev. William Johnson Fox, for the use of his congregation. In 1844 Rev. James Freeman Clarke introduced the hymn in America, but it did not gain genuine popularity until, in 1856, there was published the beautiful tune, "Bethany," which Lowell Mason wrote for it. In the Boston Peace Jubilee of 1872 the hymn was sung to this tune by nearly fifty thousand voices, and the venerable composer himself was in the audience.

Many changes have been made in the immortal hymn by the editors of hymn-books, but it is best to use it just as Mrs. Adams wrote it, which is as follows :—

> Nearer, my God, to Thee,
>   Nearer to Thee !
> E'en though it be a cross
>   That raiseth me ;
> Still all my song would be,
> Nearer, my God, to Thee,
>   Nearer to Thee !

Though like the wanderer,
    The sun gone down,
Darkness be over me,
    My rest a stone;
Yet in my dreams I'd be
Nearer, my God, to Thee,
    Nearer to Thee !

There let the way appear,
    Steps unto heaven :
All that Thou send'st to me
    In mercy given;
Angels to beckon me
Nearer, my God, to Thee,
    Nearer to Thee !

Then, with my waking thoughts
    Bright with Thy praise,
Out of my stony griefs
    Bethel I'll raise;
So by my woes to be
Nearer, my God, to Thee,
    Nearer to Thee !

Or if on joyful wing
    Cleaving the sky,
Sun, moon, and stars forgot,
    Upwards I fly,
Still all my song shall be,
Nearer, my God, to Thee,
    Nearer to Thee !

Some interesting incidents are connected with this hymn. In 1871, three eminent theologians, Professors Hitchcock, Smith, and Park, were traveling in Palestine, when they heard the strains of "Bethany."

Drawing near, to their amazement they saw fifty Syrian students standing under some trees in a circle, and singing in Arabic "Nearer, my God, to Thee." Professor Hitchcock, speaking afterward of the event, said that the singing of that Christian hymn by those Syrian youths moved him to tears, and affected him more than any singing he had ever heard before.

During the Johnstown flood, May 31, 1889, a railroad train rushed into the swirling waters. One car was turned on end, and in it was imprisoned, beyond the hope of rescue, a woman on her way to be a missionary in the far East.

She spoke to the awe-struck multitude, gazing helpless at the tragedy. Then she prayed, and finally she sung "Nearer, my God, to Thee," in which she was joined by the sorrowing, sympathizing throng. As she sung, she passed away, coming nearer indeed to the God of her worship.

But the most inspiring of all the associations of this hymn is that connected with the death of the martyred McKinley. Dr. M. D. Mann, the physician, heard him murmur among his last words, "'Nearer, my God, to Thee, E'en though it be a cross,' has been my constant prayer." On the day of his burial, Thursday, September 19, 1901, at half-past three, in all our cities and villages and wherever the daily press made way, by previous arrangement the people paused in their occupations. Trolley cars stopped. The streets were hushed. Men stood with bared heads. There were five minutes of silence over the land. In Union and Madison Squares, New York City, following this impressive silence, bands played " Nearer, my God, to Thee," and the same hymn was used in countless churches at memorial services. Among others, it was used in Westminster Abbey, at the memorial service celebrated by command of King Edward.

" Just as I Am "
Charlotte Elliott

PROBABLY no other hymn ever written has brought so many souls to Christ.

It was written by Charlotte Elliott, who was born in London, England, in 1789. She lived to be an old lady of eighty-two, but all her life she was an invalid. Her suffering made Miss Elliott most thoughtful for others in distress, and most of her hymns were written with such persons in mind. Did not God have that purpose in permitting her to become sick?

This very hymn was written when she was in great pain and trouble, and it must have helped her to take to Christ her poor, worn-out body and find the help she so much needed.

The hymn first appeared in *The Christian Remembrancer*, of which Miss Elliott became editor in 1836. Soon after it was published a lady, who admired it greatly, had it printed in leaflet form, and widely distributed. Miss Elliott was very sick, and one day her physician gave her one of these leaflets to comfort her, not knowing that she was the author. It is said that the sufferer wept tears of grateful joy when she saw this evidence that God had so used her efforts, though put forth from a feeble body.

The hymn, as first printed, had six verses. The

seventh stanza was added later, but certainly no one
would be willing to lose it.   Here is the hymn entire :—

>Just as I am, without one plea,
>But that Thy blood was shed for me,
>And that Thou bidst me come to Thee,
>>O Lamb of God, I come !

>Just as I am, and waiting not
>To rid my soul of one dark blot,
>To Thee, whose blood can cleanse each spot,
>>O Lamb of God, I come !

>Just as I am, though tossed about
>With many a conflict, many a doubt,
>Fightings and fears within, without,
>>O Lamb of God, I come !

>Just as I am, poor, wretched, blind ;
>Sight, riches, healing of the mind,
>Yea, all I need in Thee to find,
>>O Lamb of God, I come !

>Just as I am, Thou wilt receive,
>Wilt welcome, pardon, cleanse, relieve,
>Because Thy promise I believe,
>>O Lamb of God, I come !

>Just as I am, (Thy love unknown
>Has broken every barrier down),
>Now to be Thine, yea, Thine alone,
>>O Lamb of God, I come !

>Just as I am, of that free love
>The breadth, length, depth, and height to prove,
>Here for a season, then above,
>>O Lamb of God, I come !

Miss Elliott's brother, a clergyman, Rev. H. V. Elliott, once said, " In the course of a long ministry, I hope I have been permitted to see some fruit of my labors, but I feel far more has been done by a single hymn of my sister's." After the author's death more than a thousand letters were found among her papers, giving thanks for blessings received from "Just as I am." Moody once declared that no hymn has done so much good, or touched so many hearts.

For example, in the summer of 1895, the young people of the Lenox Road Methodist Church of Brooklyn sung this hymn in their service, and, as it happened, the hymn was sung also in the church service following. A few doors away lay a young lawyer in his room. All windows were open, and he heard the hymn twice repeated. At the time he was in the midst of a fierce struggle with conscience, and the hymn determined him to be a Christian.

One day Mr. Wanamaker told his great Sunday school in Philadelphia that one of their number, a young man who had been present only a week before, lay dying, and had asked the school to sing in his behalf, "Just as I am, without one plea." The hymn was sung with so much feeling, and especially the third stanza, that a visitor who was present was led to Christ, being freed on the spot from " many a conflict, many a doubt."

Once John B. Gough was placed in a pew with a man so repulsive that he moved to the farther end of the seat. The congregation began to sing "Just as I am," and the man joined in so heartily that

Mr. Gough decided that he could not be so disagree-
able after all, and moved up nearer, though the
man's singing "was positively awful."   At the end
of the third stanza, while the organ was playing the
interlude, the man leaned toward Mr. Gough and
whispered, " Won't you please give me the first line
of the next verse?"   Mr. Gough repeated,

"Just as I am, poor, wretched, blind,"

and the man replied, "That's it; and I am blind—
God help me ; and I am a paralytic."   Then as he
tried with his poor, twitching lips to make music of
the glorious words, Mr. Gough thought that never
in his life had he heard music so beautiful as the
blundering singing of that hymn by the paralytic.

"Rock of Ages"
Augustus M. Toplady

" ROCK OF AGES" and "Jesus, Lover of my soul," are the two favorite hymns of most Christians.

The author of "Rock of Ages," Augustus Montague Toplady, was an Englishman, and was born November 4, 1740. His father, Major Toplady, died in the siege of Cartagena in Colombia, South America, while his boy was only a few months old. Young Toplady was converted when on a visit to Ireland by an ignorant Methodist preacher, a layman, who was preaching in a barn.

His mind was vigorous, but his body was weak, and soon consumption seized upon him. He fought it for two years before it conquered, and it was during this period that he wrote his immortal hymn. It appeared first in the *Gospel Magazine* for March, 1776—a magazine of which he was the editor. It was in the midst of an article in which he tried to figure out the number of a man's sins, and then broke into this hymn, which sets forth our only remedy for sin : —

> Rock of Ages, cleft for me,
> Let me hide myself in Thee !
> Let the water and the blood
> From Thy riven side which flowed,
> Be of sin the double cure,
> Cleanse me from its guilt and power.

Not the labor of my hands
Can fulfil Thy law's demands ;
Could my zeal no respite know,
Could my tears forever flow,
All for sin could not atone ;
Thou must save, and Thou alone.

Nothing in my hand I bring ;
Simply to Thy cross I cling ;
Naked, come to Thee for dress ;
Helpless, look to Thee for grace ;
Foul, I to the Fountain fly ;
Wash me, Saviour, or I die.

While I draw this fleeting breath,
When my eyestrings break in death,
When I soar through tracts unknown,
See Thee on Thy judgment throne,—
Rock of Ages, cleft for me,
Let me hide myself in Thee !

Toplady's title for the hymn was " A living and
dying prayer for the holiest believer in the world."
The title fitly expressed the triumphant faith in which
he himself passed away on August 11, 1778, saying,
" My prayers are all converted into praise."   He was
only thirty-eight years old.   The hymn was actually
used as a dying prayer by Prince Albert, the beloved
husband of Queen Victoria.   It was sung in Constantinople by the Armenians during the fearful mas-
sacre.   When the steamship London went down in
the Bay of Biscay in 1866, the last man to escape

from the ill-fated vessel heard the remaining passengers singing this hymn :—

> Rock of Ages, cleft for me,
> Let me hide myself in Thee.

The hymn was an especial favorite with Gladstone, who was often heard humming it in the House of Commons, and who translated it into Latin, Greek, and Italian. His Latin translation is one of great beauty. Major-General Stuart, the famous Confederate cavalry officer, sung this hymn as he lay dying after the Battle of the Wilderness. Of many other death-beds this hymn has been the solace and the crown.

The story is told of a Chinese woman who, for the purpose of "making merit" for herself with her heathen gods, had dug a well twenty-five feet deep and fifteen in diameter. She was converted, and a traveler speaks of meeting her when she had reached the age of eighty. She was bent with age, but she stretched out her crippled hands toward her visitor, and began to sing :—

> Nothing in my hand I bring,
> Simply to Thy cross I cling.

The noblest incident connected with this hymn is related of the celebration of the fiftieth year of the reign of Queen Victoria. On this occasion there came an embassy from Queen Ranavalona III., of Madagascar, and in the company was a venerable

Hova, who expressed the desires of his people for the prosperity of the Queen, and then asked permission to sing. It was expected that he would render some heathen song, but to every one's amazement he burst forth with

> Rock of Ages, cleft for me,
> Let me hide myself in Thee.

It was a striking proof of the power of Christian missions.

"Rock of Ages" was often sung by the Armenians at Constantinople during the terrible massacres.

The hymn is given as Toplady wrote it, and it will be seen that it is often mutilated in our hymn-books. The second line of the last stanza is generally written :—

> When my eyelids close in death.

Toplady's line refers to an old belief that, when a person dies, the "eyestrings" snap.

As to the thought of "Rock of Ages," it probably sprung from the marginal translation of Isa. 26 : 4 : "In the Lord Jehovah is the rock of ages," but Toplady doubtless combined that with such passages as "I will put thee in a cleft of the rock" (Exod. 33 : 22), "Enter into the rock" (Isa. 2 : 10), and "They drank of that spiritual Rock that followed them : and that Rock was Christ" (1 Cor. 10 : 4).

Toplady wrote 133 poems and hymns, but nearly all are forgotten except this. One other, however, is

a hymn of great beauty, and is cherished by many
Christians : —

> Inspirer and Hearer of prayer,
>   Thou Shepherd and Guardian of Thine,
> My all to Thy covenant care
>   I sleeping and waking resign ;
> If Thou art my shield and my sun,
>   The night is no darkness to me ;
> And fast as my moments roll on
>   They bring me but nearer to Thee.

"Take My Life"
Frances Ridley Havergal

FRANCES RIDLEY HAVERGAL wrote so many helpful books, and lived a life so earnest and devoted, that she has had a very deep influence over the hearts of Christians. Of all her poems, the one before us meant the most to her, and has meant the most to the world.

Miss Havergal was born in Astley, England, December 14, 1836. Her father was an Episcopal clergyman, a skilful composer of music, and himself a hymn-writer. She was baptized by another hymn-writer, Rev. John Cawood, who wrote "Hark! what mean those holy voices?"

Studying in England and Germany, Miss Havergal became a good Hebrew and Greek scholar, and knew several modern languages. She became also a brilliant singer and piano-player, and a glittering career in society was open before her. But she considered all her talents to be only loans from the Lord, to be used in His service. She would not even sing, except sacred music, and for the purpose of winning souls. She lavished her strength upon work for the Master, teaching in Sunday schools, writing letters, writing many leaflets and books, conducting religious meetings, and making public addresses. She was often sick, and her life was short, but she accomplished a wonderful amount of noble work.

Miss Havergal's beautiful consecration hymn was written on February 4, 1874. Here it is.

> Take my life, and let it be
> Consecrated, Lord, to Thee.
> Take my moments and my days;
> Let them flow in ceaseless praise.
>
> Take my hands, and let them move
> At the impulse of Thy love.
> Take my feet, and let them be
> Swift and beautiful for Thee.
>
> Take my voice, and let me sing,
> Always, only, for my King.
> Take my lips, and let them be
> Filled with messages from Thee.
>
> Take my silver and my gold;
> Not a mite would I withhold.
> Take my intellect, and use
> Every power as Thou shalt choose.
>
> Take my will, and make it Thine;
> It shall be no longer mine.
> Take my heart, it is Thine own;
> It shall be Thy royal throne.
>
> Take my love; my Lord, I pour
> At Thy feet its treasure-store.
> Take myself, and I will be
> Ever, only, all for Thee.

At the close of 1873 Miss Havergal came to long for a deeper knowledge of God. On Sunday, December 2, of that year she was brought to see, as by a flash of light, that she could not have the full blessedness of a Christian without a full surrender to Christ.

On the first of February, 1874, Miss Havergal was visiting in a home where there were ten persons, some of them not converted, some of them Christians but not very happy ones. A great longing seized upon Miss Havergal that *all* of these might, before she left, come to know her Saviour as joyfully as she had just come to know Him. That prayer was granted, and before she left the house. On the last night of her stay, February 4, she was too happy to sleep, and spent the night writing this hymn, closing with the triumphant line, " *Ever*, ONLY, ALL for Thee !"

Miss Havergal made the hymn a standard for her own living. Years afterward she wrote in a letter, "I had a great time early this morning renewing the never-regretted consecration." Then she went on to tell how she found she had really made her own all but the eleventh couplet, about love ; she felt that she had not given Christ her *love* as she wanted to, and she made that the object of her morning consecration.

Sometimes the earnest worker would conduct consecration meetings, and there is an account of one such meeting in particular, at the close of which she gave each person present a card bearing the words of the hymn, and asked them to take the cards home, pray over them, and then, if they could make them their own, sign them on their knees.

This gifted and truly consecrated woman died in Wales on June 3, 1879, at the age of forty-three. She was buried at Astley, and on her tombstone is engraved, as she herself wished, her favorite text: "The blood of Jesus Christ His Son cleanseth us from all sin."

"My Faith Looks Up to Thee"

Ray Palmer

THIS is probably the greatest hymn written by an American. Its author, Ray Palmer, was the son of a judge, Hon. Thomas Palmer, and was born at Little Compton, R. I., on November 12, 1808. He became a clerk in a Boston dry-goods store, a student at Phillips Academy and at Yale, a teacher in New York and New Haven, pastor of several churches, and corresponding secretary of the American Congregational Union.

In 1830, immediately after his graduation from Yale, when Mr. Palmer was teaching in New York, he wrote his great hymn. He was then a young man of twenty-two.

"The words of the hymn," he afterward said, "were born of my own soul." He was reading, in the quiet of his own room, a brief German poem of only two stanzas, picturing a suppliant before the cross. Touched by the lines, he translated them and added four stanzas of his own—the immortal hymn :—

> My faith looks up to Thee,
> Thou Lamb of Calvary,
>   Saviour divine ;
> Now hear me while I pray,
> Take all my guilt away,
> O let me from this day
>   Be wholly Thine.

May Thy rich grace impart
Strength to my fainting heart,
  My zeal inspire;
As Thou hast died for me,
O may my love to Thee
Pure, warm, and changeless be,
  A living fire.

While life's dark maze I tread,
And griefs around me spread,
  Be Thou my Guide;
Bid darkness turn to day,
Wipe sorrow's tears away,
Nor let me ever stray
  From Thee aside.

When ends life's transient dream,
When death's cold, sullen stream
  Shall o'er me roll,
Blest Saviour, then, in love,
Fear and distrust remove;
O bear me safe above,
  A ransomed soul.

Dr. Palmer afterward said that when he was writing the last line, " A ransomed soul," " the thought that the whole work of redemption and salvation was involved in those words, and suggested the theme of eternal praises, moved the writer to a degree of emotion that brought abundant tears."

The hymn was copied into a little morocco-covered book, which Mr. Palmer carried in his pocket, reading the verses in his hours of communion with the Father. Its use as a hymn is due to a chance meeting of Mr. Palmer on a Boston street with Lowell Mason, the famous musician. He asked Mr.

Palmer for a hymn which he might use in "Spiritual Songs for Social Worship," which he was then preparing, and a copy of "My faith looks up to Thee" was at once made out in a near-by store.   Meeting the author on the street a few days later, Mr. Mason exclaimed, "You may live many years and do many good things, but I think you will be best known to posterity as the author of 'My faith looks up to Thee.'"

Of this incident Prof. Austin Phelps once wrote : " One of those fleeting conjunctions of circumstances and men !   The doctor of music and future doctor of theology are thrown together in the roaring thoroughfare of commerce for a brief interview, scarcely more than enough for a morning salutation ; and the sequence is the publication of a Christian lyric which is to be sung around the world."   The tune which Mason composed is the well-known and beautiful " Olivet," to which " My faith looks up to Thee" has always been sung.

The American publication was in 1832.   In 1842 the hymn was introduced into Great Britain, and became very popular there.   Indeed, it was not till it had received this approval over the sea that it became widely known in America.

This was Mr. Palmer's first hymn, and he afterward wrote many others, among them " Come Jesus, Redeemer, abide Thou with me " and " Take me, O my Father, take me."

His translations of Latin hymns are especially fine, the best known being " Jesus, Thou joy of loving hearts," and " Come, Holy Ghost, in love."   Mr. Palmer's own favorite among his hymns was " Jesus, these eyes have never seen." From this hymn were taken the last words the poet uttered, as, the day before he passed away, he was heard faintly murmuring the stanza :—

> " When death these mortal eyes shall seal
> And still this throbbing heart,
> The rending veil shall Thee reveal
> All glorious as Thou art."

Mr. Palmer was a man of gentle, lovable character, a saintly man, but a man of strong feeling and powerful enthusiasms.

The most touching incident connected with this great hymn is perhaps the story of eight young Christian soldiers that met for prayer in a tent just before one of the terrible battles of the Wilderness in the Civil War. They desired to write a statement which should show how they faced death and go as a comforting message to the relatives of those whom the coming battle might remove from earth. They decided to copy this hymn and sign it as their sufficient declaration of Christian faith, and they did so. On the morrow seven of those brave Union soldiers died for their country, and received in their own experience the blessed realization of the hymn's closing stanza :—

> When ends life's transient dream,
> When death's cold, sullen stream
>   Shall o'er me roll,
> Blest Saviour, then, in love,
> Fear and distrust remove ;
> O bear me safe above,
>   A ransomed soul.

"In the Cross of Christ I Glory"

Sir John Bowring

THE author of this hymn was a remarkable man, Sir John Bowring, who was born at Exeter, England, in 1792, and died in 1872. He was a very learned man. He could speak fluently twenty-two languages, and converse in one hundred. He was consul at Hong Kong, China, when the terrible Opium War broke out, and was afterward governor of that British colony. He was twice a member of the British Parliament, and he made treaties for Siam and Hawaii with six European countries. He was an ardent student of the songs of Europe, and published several volumes of translations from more than twenty languages. His little book, "Matins and Vespers," is full of beautiful religious poems. He was a sincere Christian, and lived a Christlike life. The words he wrote, "In the Cross of Christ I glory," were no unmeaning words to him, and they are fittingly cut in bold letters upon his tombstone. Sir John Bowring wrote other hymns that are often sung by all Christians. Some of these are: "God is love, His mercy brightens," "From the recesses of a lowly spirit," and "Watchman, tell us of the night." The last was written in 1825, and Bowring did not know that it was used as a hymn till ten years later, when he heard it sung in a prayer meeting of American missionaries in Asiatic Turkey.

76

But of course Bowring's most famous hymn is the following :—

> In the cross of Christ I glory,
>   Towering o'er the wrecks of time ;
> All the light of sacred story
>   Gathers round its head sublime.
>
> When the woes of life o'ertake me,
>   Hopes deceive and fears annoy,
> Never shall the cross forsake me ;
>   Lo, it glows with peace and joy.
>
> When the sun of bliss is beaming
>   Light and love upon my way,
> From the cross the radiance streaming
>   Adds new lustre to the day.
>
> Bane and blessing, pain and pleasure,
>   By the cross are sanctified :
> Peace is there that knows no measure,
>   Joys that through all time abide.
>
> In the cross of Christ I glory :
>   Towering o'er the wrecks of time,
> All the light of sacred story
>   Gathers round its head sublime.

One incident of the siege of Peking during the Boxer massacres shows the hold this hymn has upon the Christian church.   After the raising of the siege, and the terrible strain was over, the missionaries gathered in the Temple of Heaven,—that mysterious shrine which no one but the Emperor of China had been allowed to visit, and he only once a year.

Around the royal marble altar in that heathen temple gathered the missionaries of the Cross, and sang the hymn which expressed the spirit that had sustained them during those dreadful weeks of suffering and danger—"In the Cross of Christ I glory." Let us never again sing the second stanza without thinking of that inspiring scene :—

> " When the woes of life o'ertake me,
>   Hopes deceive and fears annoy,
>   Never shall the cross forsake me ;
>   Lo, it glows with peace and joy."

"Sun of My Soul"
John Keble

"THE CHRISTIAN YEAR" is one of the world's greatest books of poems. Every Christian should own it and read it. It was written by John Keble, and it is a series of poems on the different special services and saints' days of the Episcopal Church.

The book was published in 1827, and within twenty-six years forty-three editions were sold. Before the writer died, he had seen ninety-six editions, and more than half a million copies had been sold. It is still sold in large numbers.

One Sunday four travelers chanced to meet in the desert of Mount Sinai, and three of them had copies of "The Christian Year." During the Crimean War a daughter of Dr. Chalmers sent the English hospitals a whole cargo of the book.

But John Keble himself almost never read the book, and never liked to talk about it or hear it praised. He did not want to publish it, in the first place, and at last consented only on condition that his name should not appear in it. All through his life he was modest and retiring.

His life was very quiet. He was born on April 25, 1792, and died March 29, 1866. He was a remarkable scholar at Oxford, but became a country minister, and lived most of his life in charge of a village church at Hursley,—a church which he rebuilt largely out of the profits of "The Christian Year."

He was a most dutiful son and brother, a tender, loving, pure soul. The last book in his hands, before he died, was a hymn-book.

The two poems that begin "The Christian Year" have each given us a famous hymn. One is a morning hymn, beginning "New every morning is the love," and containing the famous stanza :—

> " The trivial round, the common task,
> Will furnish all we need to ask,
> Room to deny ourselves, a road
> To bring us daily nearer God."

The other is the still more famous evening hymn. The poem from which it is taken contains fourteen stanzas. The first stanza is a description of the sunset :—

> " 'Tis gone, that bright and orbèd blaze,
> Fast fading from our wistful gaze ;
> Yon mantling cloud has hid from sight
> The last faint pulse of quivering light."

But not so does the "Sun of the soul" set upon our vision. The poet goes on with the stanzas which, taken here and there from among the others, make up our hymn :—

> Sun of my soul, Thou Saviour dear,
> It is not night if Thou be near ;
> O may no earth-born cloud arise
> To hide Thee from Thy servant's eyes.

When the soft dews of kindly sleep
My wearied eyelids gently steep,
Be my last thought, how sweet to rest
For ever on my Saviour's breast.

Abide with me from morn till eve,
For without Thee I cannot live ;
Abide with me when night is nigh,
For without Thee I dare not die.

If some poor wandering child of Thine
Have spurned to-day the voice divine,
Now, Lord, the gracious work begin
Let him no more lie down in sin.

Watch by the sick ; enrich the poor
With blessings from Thy boundless store ;
Be every mourner's sleep to-night
Like infants' slumbers, pure and light.

Come near and bless us when we wake,
Ere through the world our way we take,
Till in the ocean of Thy love
We lose ourselves in heaven above.

"Am I a Soldier of the Cross?"
Isaac Watts

ISAAC WATTS, who wrote this hymn, was the father of hymn-writing in the English language, and the author of many of our greatest hymns.

He was born in Southampton, England, July 17, 1674. His father was not a member of the state church, and was twice thrown into jail for opposing it, so that when he was a baby his mother often carried him in her arms to visit his father in prison.

There are remarkable stories of young Isaac's boyhood, one of them declaring that he begged for books before he could talk plainly, and others asserting that he began Latin at the age of four and, wrote poetry at the age of seven!

He became a minister in London. He was a little man, only about five feet tall. His health was very poor all his life, but his church took loving care of him, for he was greatly liked. One day, when Watts was sick, Sir Thomas Abney invited him to his splendid home for a week. He became so dear to the household that they kept him there for the rest of his life,—thirty-six years!

Besides his preaching, Dr. Watts wrote much. He was a most zealous student of geography, astronomy, philosophy, and theology, and he wrote books on all these themes. His great life-work, however, as he himself saw, was his hymn-writing.

Early in life he became wearied with the versified Psalms which the churches used and set out to compose hymns of his own. This was a new departure and met with persistent opposition, but his hymns soon became widely popular in nearly all the churches. In 1707 Watts published his famous collection of original hymns, which he entitled "Hymns and Spiritual Songs." Only two or three copies are now in existence, and one of these sold in 1901 for $700. There were 210 hymns in this first edition, and 144 were added to the second edition.

The greatest of Watts's hymns is probably "When I survey the wondrous Cross," and many—Matthew Arnold among them—have called it the greatest hymn in the English language. Among the other great hymns of this splendid Christian poet are "Jesus shall reign where'er the sun," "Before Jehovah's awful throne," "From all that dwell below the skies," "Come, let us join our cheerful songs," "There is a land of pure delight," "Our God! our help in ages past," "Alas! and did my Saviour bleed," "Come, Holy Spirit, heavenly Dove," "Give me the wings of faith to rise." Many of Watts's children's hymns have become famous, such as "Let dogs delight to bark and bite," "How doth the little busy bee," and the sweet cradle-song, "Hush, my dear, lie still and slumber." Watts had no children of his own, but well did he know the child's heart.

The poet died November 25, 1748, and was buried at Bunhill Fields, London, near the graves of John

Bunyan and Daniel Defoe.   He is to be ranked with
Charles Wesley, the two standing together at the
summit of English sacred verse.

The noble hymn that we are to commit to memory
was written by Dr. Watts in 1709, to follow a sermon
on 1 Cor. 16 : 13, " Watch ye, stand fast in the faith,
quit you like men, be strong."   It is sometimes condensed to four stanzas, but surely we shall not wish
to lose the last two.   Here it is :—

> Am I a soldier of the cross,
>   A follower of the Lamb ?
> And shall I fear to own His cause
>   Or blush to speak His name ?
>
> Must I be carried to the skies
>   On flowery beds of ease ?
> While others fought to win the prize,
>   And sailed through bloody seas ?
>
> Are there no foes for me to face ?
>   Must I not stem the flood ?
> Is this vile world a friend to grace,
>   To help me on to God ?
>
> Sure I must fight, if I would reign ;
>   Increase my courage, Lord !
> I'll bear the toil, endure the pain,
>   Supported by Thy word.
>
> Thy saints, in all this glorious war,
>   Shall conquer, though they die ;
> They view the triumph from afar,
>   And seize it with their eye.
>
> When that illustrious day shall rise,
>   And all Thy armies shine
> In robes of victory through the skies,
>   The glory shall be Thine.

"Stand Up, Stand Up for Jesus!"
George Duffield

IN the spring of 1858 there was a great revival in Philadelphia, and one of the leaders of it was an earnest, manly young minister, not quite thirty years old, named Dudley A. Tyng. One day Mr. Tyng's arm got caught in some machinery and fearfully torn. The arm was amputated, but in a few days the noble young man died of his injuries.

As he was dying he sent a message to the ministers who had worked with him in the revival, and the message began with these words: "Tell them, 'Let us all stand up for Jesus.'" The words made a deep impression. They were quoted often before large assemblies, and they were made the basis of more than one poem.

Among Mr. Tyng's most devoted friends was Rev. George Duffield. A few weeks after the sad accident he preached in his own church in Philadelphia, taking as his text Eph. 6 : 14, "Stand, therefore, having your loins girt about with truth, and having on the breastplate of righteousness"; and closing his sermon with the hymn which he had just written, "Stand up, stand up for Jesus." The song at once became popular, was introduced into the hymnbooks, and became an especial favorite of the soldiers during the Civil War.

Here is the hymn just as Mr. Duffield wrote it,

including the two stanzas that are now never printed :—

Stand up, stand up for Jesus,
Ye soldiers of the cross ;
Lift high His royal banner,
It must not suffer loss :
From victory unto victory
His army He shall lead,
Till every foe is vanquished,
And Christ is Lord indeed.

[Stand up, stand up for Jesus,
The solemn watchword hear ;
If while ye sleep He suffers,
Away with shame and fear ;
Where'er ye meet with evil,
Within you or without,
Charge for the God of Battles,
And put the foe to rout.]

Stand up, stand up for Jesus,
The trumpet call obey ;
Forth to the mighty conflict
In this His glorious day :
Ye that are men now serve Him
Against unnumbered foes ;
Let courage rise with danger,
And strength to strength oppose.

Stand up, stand up for Jesus,
Stand in His strength alone.
The arm of flesh will fail you,
Ye dare not trust your own :
Put on the gospel armor,
Each piece put on with prayer ;
Where duty calls, or danger,
Be never wanting there.

[Stand up, stand up for Jesus,
  Each soldier to his post;
Close up the broken column,
  And shout through all the host:
Make good the loss so heavy,
  In those that still remain,
And prove to all around you
  That death itself is gain.]

Stand up, stand up for Jesus,
  The strife will not be long;
This day the noise of battle,
  The next the victor's song:
To him that overcometh
  A crown of life shall be;
He with the King of Glory
  Shall reign eternally.

Mr. Duffield was the father of a poet, Rev. Samuel W. Duffield. He was a Presbyterian, and during his long life (1818 to 1888) he served Christ faithfully in many churches; but probably the most fruitful of all his labors was the writing of this hymn, which has inspired so many to speak and act boldly for their Saviour.

The reference, in the second stanza, to the disciples' sleeping in Gethsemane, recalls a sermon preached from that passage by Mr. Tyng during the revival, not long before his death. Note especially also the sixth line of stanza four, which is often changed (foolishly) to " And, watching unto prayer."

"Onward, Christian Soldiers"
Sabine Baring-Gould

THIS stirring poem is the chief marching hymn in the English language. It was written very hastily one evening by a remarkable man, Rev. Sabine Baring-Gould, then curate of an Episcopal church at Horbury, Yorkshire, England. It was the day before the Whitmonday holiday, in 1865. The children of his village school were to march to the next village and meet there the children of another school. No good song could be found for them to sing while marching, and it was to meet this emergency that the hymn was written.

It had originally six stanzas, as follows :—

> Onward, Christian soldiers,
>   Marching as to war,
> With the cross of Jesus
>   Going on before :
> Christ the Royal Master
>   Leads against the foe ;
> Forward into battle,
>   See, His banners go.

> Onward, Christian soldiers,
>   Marching as to war,
> With the cross of Jesus
>   Going on before.

At the sign of triumph
    Satan's host doth flee;
On then, Christian soldiers,
    On to victory:
Hell's foundations quiver
    At the shout of praise;
Brothers, lift your voices,
    Loud your anthems raise.

Onward, etc.

Like a mighty army
    Moves the Church of God;
Brothers, we are treading
    Where the saints have trod;
We are not divided,
    All one body we,
One in hope and doctrine,
    One in charity.

Onward, etc.

What the saints established
    That I hold for true,
What the saints believèd
    That believe I too.
Long as earth endureth
    Men that Faith will hold,—
Kingdoms, nations, empires,
    In destruction rolled.

Onward, etc.

Crowns and thrones may perish,
    Kingdoms rise and wane,
But the Church of Jesus
    Constant will remain;

Gates of hell can never
　'Gainst that Church prevail ;
We have Christ's own promise,
　And that cannot fail.

Onward, etc.

Onward, then, ye people,
　Join our happy throng,
Blend with ours your voices
　In the triumph-song ;
Glory, laud, and honor
　Unto Christ the King ;
This through countless ages
　Men and angels sing.

Onward, etc.

The fourth stanza is now never printed, and is plainly inferior to the others ; the second stanza is rarely seen.

Very soon the hymn appeared in our country, and the martial spirit engendered by our Civil War was, as Dr. Benson thinks, the cause of its immediate and great popularity. This popularity was augmented by the splendid tune written for the hymn in 1871 by Arthur S. Sullivan, the tune to which it is universally sung.

Mr. Baring-Gould was born in 1834 (January 28), and is still living, being rector of Lew Trenchard, Devonshire,—a "living" within the gift of his family, to which he presented himself in 1881. He is the owner of 3,000 acres of land, inherited through three centuries of ancestors. He holds the important office of justice of the peace (more important in England than in the United States).

Mr. Baring-Gould is one of the most versatile and industrious of men. His "Lives of the Saints" is in fifteen volumes. His "Curious Myths of the Middle Ages" is a famous work; so is his "Legends of the Old Testament." He has written a large number of learned books, besides many devotional writings and volumes of sermons. In addition, he is one of the most popular of English novelists, regularly producing one novel a year. An incomplete list of his works that lies before me includes seventy-three titles. All this work has been done with the pen, without the aid of a secretary, and Mr. Baring-Gould gives as the sufficient secret of his accomplishments the fact that when he has begun a task, he sticks to it till it is finished. He often does his best work, he says, when he feels least like working, and he never waits for "inspiration," but plunges determinedly at his work.

"Onward, Christian soldiers" is not by any means the only famous hymn Mr. Baring-Gould has written. Others from his graceful and vigorous pen are "Now the day is over," and "Through the night of doubt and shadow."

"Awake, My Soul"
Bishop Thomas Ken

THE first great hymn-writer of England was the good Bishop Thomas Ken, who lived during the times of Cromwell and the kings that followed him. He was born in 1637, and died in 1711, after a long and troubled life, in which he took the part of a hero.

His mother died when he was a child, and he was brought up by his brother-in-law, that famous and pure-hearted angler, Izaak Walton. He went to school, therefore, at Winchester, and his name may still be seen there, cut in one of the stone pillars. He graduated from Oxford.

In 1679, the wife of William of Orange, the niece of the English king, asked for a chaplain, and Charles II. sent Thomas Ken to the Hague. But Ken had a dispute there, because he was too bold in rebuking some corruption in the court, and he left the Hague in 1680. Then Charles made him one of his own chaplains.

Once more he lived in Winchester, and in 1683 King Charles came there and asked Ken to give up his house temporarily for the accommodation of a certain dissolute woman who was with the King. "Not for the King's kingdom," was Ken's prompt and unflinching reply.

Charles had sense enough to see that such a man was worth while, and the next year, when the bishopric of Bath and Wells became vacant, he asked: " Where is the little man who wouldn't give poor Nell a lodging? Give it to him." And so Thomas Ken became a bishop.

But Charles II. died soon after, and the uncompromising character of Ken soon got him into trouble again with the court. In 1688 he so offended James II. that he was sent to the Tower, but he was soon afterward acquitted. When William III. came to the throne, the heroic clergyman was deposed from his bishopric, and though Queen Anne received him back again into partial favor, and gave him a pension of a thousand dollars a year, he was not restored to his place as a bishop. However, the last years of his life were peaceful, and he died serenely.

Bishop Ken, though he wrote many hymns, and wished his hymns to live on the lips of all succeeding generations, penned only three hymns that are now in common use. These three, however, are great compositions, and one of them, the "long-metre Doxology," "Praise God from whom all blessings flow," is more often repeated by bodies of Christians than any other set of words except the Lord's Prayer.

The other two hymns that have become famous are the morning hymn here given, and the evening hymn beginning, "Glory to Thee, my God, this night." The four lines of the immortal Doxology were originally printed at the close of both the morning and the evening hymns.

Awake, my soul, and with the sun
Thy daily stage of duty run ;
Shake off dull sloth, and joyful rise
To pay thy morning sacrifice.

Awake, lift up thyself, my heart,
And with the angels bear thy part,
Who all night long unwearied sing
High praises to the eternal King.

Glory to Thee, who safe hast kept,
And hast refreshed me while I slept ;
Grant, Lord, when I from death shall wake,
I may of endless life partake.

Lord, I my vows to Thee renew :
Scatter my sins as morning dew ;
Guard my first springs of thought and will,
And with Thyself my spirit fill.

Direct, control, suggest this day,
All I design, or do, or say ;
That all my powers, with all their might,
In Thy sole glory may unite.

"Abide with Me"
Henry Francis Lyte

HENRY FRANCIS LYTE, the author of this, one of the greatest of all hymns, was born June 1, 1793, at Ednam, near Kelso, Scotland, where also was born the poet James Thomson, author of "The Seasons." He was early left an orphan, and in comparative poverty. Three times in college his poems won him prizes At first he intended to be a physician, but fortunately he became a clergyman of the Church of England.

One day, in Cornwall, a brother clergyman, on his death-bed, sent to Lyte that the young man might give him spiritual comfort. To their mutual grief, they found themselves groping for the light, veritable blind guides. Their search led them into confident certainty, and Lyte emerged from that sick-room a changed man.

It was this experience, it is said, that prompted Lyte's noble hymn, "Jesus, I my cross have taken."

He took charge, in 1823, of a seashore parish, Lower Brixham, in Devonshire. There, amid rough seafaring men, he toiled for twenty-four years, till his death. He gathered a Sunday school of several hundred scholars, and trained a splendid company of seventy or eighty teachers. For this church he wrote nearly all his hymns.

But "the sword was too sharp for the scabbard."

Ever of delicate health and threatened with consumption, he became obliged to spend his winters in the warmth of southern Europe.

Greatly weakened, on the fourth of September, 1847, he was about to leave England for this purpose when he was seized with an irresistible desire to preach to his people once more. Against the protest of his amazed friends, he accomplished this purpose. "O brethren," he said, as he entered the familiar pulpit for the last time, "I stand here among you to-day, as alive from the dead, if I may hope to impress it upon you, and induce you to prepare for that solemn hour which must come to all, by a timely acquaintance with the death of Christ." He closed his service by administering to his weeping people the Holy Communion.

That evening the impulse to poetical composition came upon him, and he wrote his last and greatest hymn :—

> Abide with me : fast falls the eventide ;
> The darkness deepens ; Lord, with me abide :
> When other helpers fail, and comforts flee,
> Help of the helpless, O abide with me.
>
> Swift to its close ebbs out life's little day ;
> Earth's joys grow dim, its glories pass away ;
> Change and decay in all around I see ;
> O Thou who changest not, abide with me.
>
> Not a brief glance I beg, a passing word ;
> But, as Thou dwell'st with Thy disciples, Lord,
> Familiar, condescending, patient, free,
> Come, not to sojourn, but abide, with me.

Come not in terrors, as the King of kings ;
But kind and good, with healing in Thy wings ;
Tears for all woes, a heart for every plea ;
Come, Friend of sinners, and thus 'bide with me.

Thou on my head in early youth didst smile ;
And, though rebellious and perverse meanwhile,
Thou hast not left me, oft as I left Thee :
On to the close, O Lord, abide with me.

I need Thy presence every passing hour ;
What but Thy grace can foil the tempter's power ?
Who like Thyself my guide and stay can be ?
Through cloud and sunshine, O abide with me.

I fear no foe, with Thee at hand to bless :
Ills have no weight, and tears no bitterness.
Where is death's sting ? where, grave, thy victory ?
I triumph still, if Thou abide with me.

Hold Thou Thy cross before my closing eyes ;
Shine through the gloom, and point me to the skies :
Heaven's morning breaks, and earth's vain shadows flee :
In life, in death, O Lord, abide with me.

This hymn he handed to a member of his family that very night. Setting out the next day, Lyte reached Nice, where he died on November 20 of the same year, 1847, his last words being "Joy! Peace!" There his body lies, the grave marked simply by that cross which he named in the last stanza of his immortal lyric.

Thus "Abide with me" was written in the shadows of death. Moreover, Mr. Lyte had been having some trouble with his people, and it is said that the words,

"When other helpers fail," were prompted by the
estrangement of some of his helpers in the church.

In an earlier poem, "Declining Days," Lyte had
longed to leave behind him

> "Some simple strain, some spirit-moving lay,
>   Some sparklet of the Soul that still might live
>   When I was passed to clay."

In the closing stanza he had prayed :

> "O Thou ! whose touch can lend
> Life to the dead, Thy quick'ning grace supply,
> And grant me, swanlike, my last breath to spend
>   In song that may not die ! "

Truly that prayer was answered. Few swan
songs in all earth's history have been so honored by
God and man.

The hymn was based, of course, on the scene at
Emmaus, and the words (Luke 24 : 29), "Abide with
us : for it is toward evening, and the day is far
spent." It is not, however, an evening hymn; for
the evening thought of by the poet in his hymn was
the twilight of life, the night of death.

Of the eight verses originally written, and given
above, the third, fourth, and fifth are usually omitted
from our hymn-books. Contrary to the usual result
in such condensations, there is here a gain in force,
as most readers will feel. All, however, will wish to
preserve the entire hymn.

Lyte himself composed a tune for this hymn on
the same evening when he wrote it, but the tune

that is universally used with it was written by Dr. William Henry Monk, a noted London musician, in 1861. The tune was composed in ten minutes, to fill a blank in a hymn-book.

Among Lyte's other hymns the best known are "Pleasant are thy courts above," "As pants the hart for cooling streams," and "Praise, my soul, the King of heaven." "In no other writer," says Dr. Breed, "are poetry and religion more exquisitely united."

"God Be with You Till We Meet Again"
J. E. Rankin

THIS beautiful benediction hymn is known all the world around. It has closed, with its sweet strains of Christian farewell, religious meetings beyond number.

The hymn was written in 1882 by Rev. Jeremiah Eames Rankin, D. D., LL. D., who was at that time pastor of the First Congregational Church of Washington, D. C. It was written to interpret the familiar words, " good-by," which are merely a contraction of the sentence, " God be with you," and it was composed as a Christian benediction hymn, without being intended for any special occasion. Here is the poem entire. The first, second, fourth, and seventh stanzas are all that are commonly sung :

God be with you till we meet again,
   By His counsels guide, uphold you ;
   With His sheep securely fold you ;
God be with you till we meet again.

God be with you till we meet again,
   'Neath His wings protecting hide you ;
   Daily manna still divide you ;
God be with you till we meet again.

God be with you till we meet again,
   With the oil of joy anoint you ;
   Sacred ministries appoint you ;
God be with you till we meet again.

God be with you till we meet again,
  When life's perils thick confound you,
  Put His arms unfailing round you ;
God be with you till we meet again.

God be with you till we meet again,
  Of His promises remind you ;
  For life's upper garner bind you ;
God be with you till we meet again.

God be with you till we meet again,
  Sicknesses and sorrows taking,
  Never leaving nor forsaking ;
God be with you till we meet again.

God be with you till we meet again,
  Keep love's banner floating o'er you ;
  Smite death's threat'ning wave before you ;
God be with you till we meet again.

God be with you till we meet again.
  Ended when for you earth's story,
  Israel's chariot sweep to glory ;
God be with you till we meet again.

CHORUS :
  Till we meet at Jesus' feet,
  God be with you till we meet again.

I copy the poem from Dr. Rankin's own book, giving the form he preferred. He objected very strongly, and quite properly, to the changes introduced by the hymn-tinkers, such as, " Put His *loving* arms around you," " Daily manna still *provide* you," and the repetition in the chorus, " Till we meet *again.*" These changes transformed the thought, and are certainly the reverse of an improvement.

Wherever Christian Endeavor has gone this hymn has been adopted, and it has been translated into many tongues. Not only have Christian Endeavorers come to love the song, but it has been adopted by the Woman's Christian Temperance Union as the benediction song of that organization also. It has been sung on many other farewell occasions, as, for example, in Memphis ten years ago, when a company of three thousand persons, bidding farewell to President Roosevelt, broke out spontaneously with the familiar "God be with you till we meet again."

The music for this famous hymn was composed, at Dr. Rankin's request, by William Gould Tomer, at that time a school-teacher in Carpentersville, N. J. Mr. Tomer's music was slightly revised by Dr. J. W. Bischoff, the blind organist of Dr. Rankin's church. It was sung in that church for the first time. It is an interesting fact that Mr. Tomer was a Methodist, and that the Methodists at Ocean Grove first made the hymn popular.

Dr. Rankin was descended from the Scotch Covenanters. He was the cousin of Melinda Rankin, the stout-hearted pioneer missionary to Mexico. He was born at Thornton, N. H., January 2, 1828, and died at Cleveland, O., November 28, 1904, aged nearly seventy-seven years. His long and useful life included about thirty-five years as a pastor, and about seven years as professor and president at Howard University, that noble institution for colored people, situated in Washington.

Dr. Rankin wrote many poems, and published a volume of hymns.   Among his hymns that have become especially famous is,

> " Out of my darkness into Thy light,
> Out of my weakness into Thy might,
> Jesus, I come; Jesus, I come."

The well-known Christian Endeavor hymn, " Keep Your Colors Flying," was written for the Fifth International Christian Endeavor Convention, at Saratoga, where it was first sung.   Dr. Rankin was one of the speakers at that convention, and was from the start deeply interested in Christian Endeavor.   Writing concerning his famous benediction hymn, he once said: " It has had no sweeter recognition than that given it by its adoption by the Young People's Society of Christian Endeavor.   Long, long, may they sing it!"

"O Day of Rest and Gladness"
Bishop Wordsworth

CHRISTOPHER WORDSWORTH, who wrote this beautiful hymn of the Lord's Day, was a nephew of the great poet, William Wordsworth, and his biographer. He was born in England in 1807, and died in 1885.

When a lad, he was athletic, and a famous scholar. At the early age of thirty he won a splendid position, becoming head of the school at Harrow. In 1844 he was made Canon of Westminster Abbey, and opposed the appointment of Dr. Arthur Stanley as dean, because of Stanley's liberal views. In 1869 he became Bishop of Lincoln, and labored most successfully in that position till his death.

Bishop Wordsworth was a notable scholar, and wrote many books, especially an important work on Greece, and a learned commentary on the Bible. He wrote also many hymns, 127 in all, which he placed in a hymn-book called "The Holy Year," published in 1862. These hymns were written to illustrate his theory that hymns should not deal with personal, individual interests, but that they should teach the truths of Scripture, and voice the worship of the whole congregation.

The first hymn of the book—almost the only hymn of Wordsworth's that is well known or much

used—is the beautiful lyric we are studying.   It is
printed here just as it was written, but in our hymn-
books the fourth stanza is always omitted, as distinctly inferior to the others.

> O day of rest and gladness,
>   O day of joy and light,
> O balm of care and sadness,
>   Most beautiful, most bright ;
> On thee the high and lowly,
>   Through ages join in tune,
> Sing Holy, Holy, Holy,
>   To the great God Triune.
>
> On thee, at the creation,
>   The light first had its birth ;
> On thee, for our salvation,
>   Christ rose from depths of earth ;
> On thee our Lord, victorious,
>   The Spirit sent from heaven ;
> And thus on thee, most glorious,
>   A triple light was given.
>
> Thou art a port protected
>   From storms that round us rise ;
> A garden intersected
>   With streams of Paradise ;
> Thou art a cooling fountain
>   In life's dry, dreary sand ;
> From thee, like Pisgah's mountain,
>   We view our promised land.
>
> Thou art a holy ladder,
>   Where angels go and come ;
> Each Sunday finds us gladder,
>   Nearer to Heaven, our home.

A day of sweet reflection
   Thou art, a day of love;
A day of Resurrection
   From earth to heaven above.

To-day on weary nations
   The heavenly manna falls:
To holy convocations
   The silver trumpet calls,
Where gospel light is glowing
   With pure and radiant beams,
And living water flowing
   With soul-refreshing streams.

New graces ever gaining
   From this our day of rest,
We reach the rest remaining
   To spirits of the blest.
To Holy Ghost be praises,
   To Father, and to Son;
The Church her voice upraises
   To Thee, blest Three in One.

" In This Consecration Hour "

Howard Benjamin Grose

D R. HOWARD BENJAMIN GROSE is the son of a Baptist minister who was also the editor and publisher of a village paper, and at nine years of age the boy was put to work by his father in a printing-office. He followed the printer's trade until he reached the age of seventeen, learning thoroughly all parts of the fascinating work, from the miscellaneous jobs of the " devil " to the doing of job printing.

He had altogether less than two years of regular schooling, but in the evenings he studied Latin, Greek, and mathematics with the help of an Episcopal rector who afterward became Bishop Worthington.

At the age of nineteen the ambitious young man was able to enter college, at first paying his way by typesetting, and in his freshman year by newspaper reporting. He was graduated from Rochester University in 1876, and became associate editor of *The New York Examiner.*

Then, in 1883, he was called to the pastorate of the First Baptist Church of Poughkeepsie, N. Y. While there he saw an item describing the new young people's society in Portland, Me., and wrote to Dr. Clark, the pastor of the church, receiving from him a copy of the Christian Endeavor constitution.

At once Mr. Grose organized a Christian Endeavor society, one of the earliest to be formed. This society is strong to-day, and through all these years it has been a mainstay of the church.

Removing to Pittsburg, Penn., as pastor of the Fourth Avenue Baptist Church, Mr. Grose organized a society there. From Pittsburg he was called to the presidency of the South Dakota University, and thence to the new University of Chicago during its organization period.

Drawn to New England in 1896, he became associate editor of *The Watchman* of Boston, and later he was chosen editorial secretary of the American Baptist Home Mission Society, with headquarters in New York City.

As editor of *The Baptist Home Mission Monthly* he made a publication unexcelled for enterprise, brilliancy, and effectiveness, and when the Baptists decided to have one missionary magazine for both home and foreign work, Dr. Grose was made its editor, and the new magazine, *Missions*, has set a new standard for missionary periodicals.

Dr. Grose began writing very early. Converted at the age of twelve, he was intrusted by his father with the editing of a religious column in his father's weekly paper. At the type-case he began original composition, sometimes filling his column with paragraph sermons.

He has become a skilled and exceedingly attractive

writer, his most notable book being the text-book on immigration, "Aliens or Americans?" written for the Young People's Missionary Movement, of whose central board he is a member. This is a fascinating text-book, and has had a phenomenal sale.

It was followed by the home-mission-study text-book, "Advance in the Antilles," an equally strong contribution to the literature of missions, which gathers up the observations made by Dr. Grose in his visits to the West Indies.

Dr. Grose's degree of doctor of divinity was conferred upon him in 1907 by Brown University. Deeply interested in the cause of Christian unity, he has served as chairman of the business committee of the Federal Council of Churches, and is also a member of its commission on social service.

Dr. Grose, accompanied by a delegate, went to the Old Orchard Convention of Christian Endeavor societies in 1885, and was elected one of the original trustees of the United Society of Christian Endeavor, an office which he still holds, being the vice-president of the United Society. He organized the New York State Christian Endeavor Union, and was its first president, serving for two terms. When in Pittsburg he organized the Pittsburg Union, which became one of the strongest of the Christian Endeavor local unions.

Dr. Grose designed the Christian Endeavor monogram pin, which is now to be seen in all parts of the world. He has spoken hundreds of times in all kinds of Christian Endeavor conventions, from the local gatherings to the great world's conventions.

Among Dr. Grose's many contributions to the cause of Christian Endeavor his musical services have been valuable and prominent. He was one of the most active editors of " The Endeavor Hymnal " and of " The Praise Book," and he is especially interested in elevating young people's taste in the matter of hymns. He is himself a writer of verse of much merit, and has a keen sense of strong musical composition.

As to this consecration hymn, " In This Consecration Hour," Dr. Grose says that it was not born of special inspiration or unusual circumstances, but sprung from a pastor's conscious need of more consecration hymns for the Christian Endeavor consecration meetings. The familiar hymns are good, but too few, necessitating too frequent repetition. It seemed to him also that the note of consecration might profitably be linked to service and purpose, rather than merely to the idea of surrender. In response to that need and mood the words came, and were written expressly for the tune, " Blumenthal," which seems admirably fitted for such a theme. This is the hymn :—

In this consecration hour,
  Lord, I lift my soul to Thee ;
Visit me in saving power,
  From myself, O, set me free.
Hear, O God, my earnest prayer,
For Thy work my soul prepare,
In Thy service give me share ;
  Hearken, Father, to my plea.

As in penitence I bow,
  Love divine to me reveal ;
As I here renew my vow,
  Fill me, Lord, with holy zeal.
Hear me, Father, as I pray,
Grace bestow for each new day,
Keep me near Thee all the way ;
  Hear, O Father, my appeal.

"Blest Be the Tie That Binds"
John Fawcett

THE author of this favorite hymn, one of the most commonly used of all our Christian songs, was John Fawcett, who was born on January 17, 1739, at Lidget Green, Yorkshire, England.

When he was thirteen years old he was apprenticed to a London tailor, and remained with him through his period of apprenticeship, which was six years.

At the age of sixteen he was converted by a sermon preached by the famous evangelist, George Whitefield, the text being John 3 : 14, and in 1765 he was ordained as a Baptist minister, and soon obtained a small church at Wainsgate in Yorkshire. Here he remained for the rest of his life, serving his people with great fidelity.

In 1772 he was called to become the pastor of a famous Baptist church in London.

He accepted the call, preached his farewell sermon, and had already placed his household goods upon wagons when the love and the tears of his people gathered around him prevailed, and he found it impossible to leave them.

It was within a week, while the memory of this affecting scene was fresh upon him, that he wrote this hymn of Christian fellowship, " Blest be the tie that binds."

Though his position gave him a salary of less than $200 a year, and though he received other invitations to fields that were more attractive from a worldly point of view, he accepted none of them.

In 1811 he received the degree of doctor of divinity from Brown University in the United States.

He died on July 25, 1817, at the age of seventy-eight. His last words were, " Come, Lord Jesus, come quickly."

Dr. Fawcett wrote many prose religious works, and six volumes of poems. In 1780 his address on " Anger " was presented to George III., and it found so great favor with the monarch that he offered to give the writer any favor he might ask.

Dr. Fawcett did not accept the kindness at the time, but later, when the son of one of his intimate friends was convicted of forgery, and, in accordance with the laws of the times, was sentenced to be hung, he besought pardon for him from the king, and in memory of his book he obtained it.

In 1782 he issued a volume containing 166 hymns. Most of these hymns he composed at midnight on Saturday to be sung after his sermon on the following day. Among the most famous of his hymns are, " How precious is the Book Divine," " Thus far my God hath led me on," " Praise to Thee, thou great Creator," and " Thy way, O God, is in the sea." Many think that he also wrote the hymn, " Lord, dismiss us with Thy blessing," the authorship of which is uncertain.

But of all his hymns by far the most famous is " Blest be the tie that binds." Instances of its use on notable occasions are very numerous. A famous example is the story of the missionary, Coffin, who, in 1860, left his station at Aintab, Turkey, to explore a dangerous and distant region of the Taurus Mountains. His loving Armenian converts, to the number of 1,500, expecting not to see his face again, gathered on the road over which he was to pass, and as their farewell sang, " Blest be the tie."

When Moody was a Sunday-school superintendent in Chicago, one of his teachers who had a class of girls learned that he was threatened with a fatal disease and must leave the city.

Conscience-stricken because he had not sought earnestly for the conversion of his class, he got Mr. Moody to accompany him, and in a carriage for ten days they visited the girls, until finally every one of them had accepted Christ.

The farewell meeting at the house of this faithful teacher was profoundly affecting, and as they tried to sing in parting, " Blest be the tie that binds," they were all so moved that they broke down.

Probably the most notable occasion of the use of this hymn was at the famous gathering in Pittsburg in November, 1869, when the two divisions of the Presbyterian Church, the Old and the New Schools, came together after many years of separation. On the consummation of this union " Blest be the tie " was sung by the large assembly.

During recent years this hymn has been constantly used in the international Christian Endeavor Con-

ventions.   Almost always at some time during the
Convention the American national hymn, "My
country, 'tis of thee," and the British national
hymn, "God save the King," are sung, and are
immediately followed by "Blest be the tie that
binds."

This sequence of hymns was most impressively
sung at the World's Christian Endeavor Convention
in London in 1900, and at the close of the Convention, when a large party of Christian Endeavorers
was received by Queen Victoria at Windsor Castle,
after singing "God save the Queen," the Endeavorers followed it with "Blest be the tie that binds."

In the church of which the founder of Christian
Endeavor, Dr. F. E. Clark, is a member, in Auburn-
dale, Mass., every Friday-night church prayer meeting is closed by the singing of the opening stanza of
this hymn :—

> Blest be the tie that binds
>   Our hearts in Christian love ;
> The fellowship of kindred minds
>   Is like to that above.

> Before our Father's throne
>   We pour our ardent prayers ;
> Our fears, our hopes, our aims are one,
>   Our comforts and our cares.

> We share our mutual woes,
>   Our mutual burdens bear ;
> And often for each other flows
>   The sympathizing tear.

When we asunder part,
　　It gives us inward pain ;
But we shall still be joined in heart,
　　And hope to meet again.

This glorious hope revives
　　Our courage by the way ;
While each in expectation lives,
　　And longs to see the day.

From sorrow, toil, and pain,
　　And sin, we shall be free,
And perfect love and friendship reign
　　Through all eternity.

"If You Cannot on the Ocean"
Ellen M. Huntington Gates

MRS. ELLEN M. HUNTINGTON GATES, the wife of Isaac G. Gates, and the youngest sister of the famous financier, Collis P. Huntington, was born in Torrington, Conn. One afternoon in the winter of 1860, according to her own account (Hezekiah Butterworth, whose story of this hymn is fuller than that of any other, says that it was in the winter of 1861 and 1862), she was looking through the window at the falling snow when there came to her mind the beautiful hymn, "If you cannot on the ocean." "It wrote itself," she afterward declared, "and I knew, as I know now, that the poem was only a simple little thing, but somehow I had a presentiment that it had wings and would fly into sorrowful hearts, uplifting and strengthening them."

She wrote the poem on her slate, and, having written it, fell on her knees and consecrated it to a divine purpose. She sent free copies to a local paper of Cooperstown, N. Y., and also to the Baptist paper, the New York *Examiner*, and it was published in both of these periodicals.

The hymn was made famous by the following incident.

In February, 1865, there was a great meeting of the United States Christian Commission, an organization for the care of the soldiers when they were sick and for other helpful ministries. The meeting was in the Senate chamber, and Lincoln was there, together with Secretary Seward, who was then the president of the Christian Commission. The hall was crowded with distinguished soldiers and civilians.

As part of the exercises Philip Phillips sang Mrs. Gates's hymn, "Your Mission." It made a deep impression, especially in the fifth stanza, "If you cannot in the conflict," etc., so beautifully appropriate to the occasion. President Lincoln wrote hastily upon a scrap of paper which he sent to Secretary Seward near the close, "Let us have 'Your Mission' repeated."

It is said that Mr. Phillips was so moved by his success on this occasion that he was led by the event to give up everything in order to adopt the calling of a gospel singer. He was a pioneer in this work, and it was his example that led Sankey to give up his business as a revenue officer and devote his life to the ministry of sacred song. All of this can be traced back directly to Mrs. Gates's beautiful hymn.

Mrs. Gates published a number of volumes of poems, including "Treasures of Kurium," and "The Dark: To the Unborn Peoples."

She lived in Elizabeth, N. J., when she wrote this hymn, but lives now in New York City.

Other famous hymns have come from her pen— "Come home! come home! you are weary at heart," "I will sing you a song of that beautiful land," "I am now a child of God," "O, the clanging bells of time," "Say, is your lamp burning, my brother?"

I give the hymn entire, though it is not so printed in our hymnals:—

If you cannot on the ocean
  Sail among the swiftest fleet,
Rocking on the highest billow,
  Laughing at the storms you meet,
You can stand among the sailors
  Anchored yet within the bay,
You can lend a hand to help them
  As they launch their boats away.

If you are too weak to journey
  Up the mountain steep and high,
You can stand within the valley,
  Where the multitudes go by.
You can chant in happy measure,
  As they slowly pass along;
Though they may forget the singer,
  They will not forget the song.

If you cannot, in the harvest,
  Gather up the richest sheaves,—
Many a grain both ripe and golden
  Oft the careless reaper leaves,—
Go and glean among the briars
  Growing rank against the wall,
For it may be that their shadow
  Hides the heaviest wheat of all.

If you have not gold and silver
  Ever ready to command,
If you cannot toward the needy
  Reach an ever-open hand,
You can visit the afflicted,
  O'er the erring you can weep ;
With the Saviour's true disciples
  You a patient watch may keep.

If you cannot in the conflict
   Prove yourself a soldier true,
If, where fire and smoke are thickest,
   There's no work for you to do,
When the battle-field is silent
   You can go with careful tread,
You can bear away the wounded,
   You can cover up the dead.

Do not, then, stand idly waiting
   For some greater work to do;
Fortune is a lazy goddess,
   She will never come to you.
Go and toil in any vineyard;
   Do not fear to do or dare;
If you want a field of labor
   You can find it anywhere.

"Art Thou Weary, Art Thou Languid?"
John Mason Neale

THERE are few dialogue hymns, and of those few this is one of the very best. It was written by John Mason Neale, D. D., who was born in London, January 24, 1818.

His father died when the boy was five years old, and young Neale was trained by his mother,—"a mother," as he said not long before his death, "to whom I owe more than I can express." The lad went to Cambridge University, and was the best scholar in his class. One of the university prizes he won eleven times.

In 1840 Neale became a minister of the Church of England. He was a man of mystical temperament, more like a monk of the Middle Ages than like a modern Englishman, and he became one of the most advanced ritualists in the church. He founded a sisterhood, St. Margaret's, which was, and is, devoted to charity.

His practices were so close to Roman Catholicism that he aroused much popular prejudice. At one time he was attacked by a mob as he was attending the funeral of one of the sisters of St. Margaret, concerning whom the absurd rumor was that he had caused her to contract scarlet fever in order to obtain her money. At one time his bishop suspended

121

him from pastoral functions for fourteen years, and some of the religious establishments that he founded had to be given up. For many years before his death he was merely the warden of Sackville College, an obscure almshouse, on a salary of $135 a year. He continued, however, true to his beliefs, and he was so kind and lovable and charitable toward all that he lived down the prejudice against himself. He passed away on August 6, 1866.

Dr. Neale was a remarkable scholar, learned in other languages, and skilful in the use of English. There is a story that at one time, when John Keble was visiting him, Dr. Neale excused himself and went into another room for a few minutes, and upon his return said, with an expression of surprise, " I thought, Keble, that all your poems in ' The Christian Year ' were original ; but one of them, at least, seems to be a translation." With this he handed Keble, to the amazement of the poet, an admirable translation into Latin of one of Keble's own poems, a translation which Dr. Neale had made during his few minutes' absence in the other room.

Dr. Neale was particularly fond of the songs of the old monks written in Greek and Latin, and he did more than any one else to make them known to the present world. Among his translations from these ancient Latin hymns are the famous " Jerusalem, the golden," " For thee, O dear, dear country," and " Brief life is here our portion." Among his translations from the Greek are " Christian, dost thou see them," " The day is past and over," and " A day of resurrection." Perhaps the best known of his original hymns is "Holy Father, Thou hast taught me." He published many volumes in prose as well as many in verse.

The hymn, "Art thou weary, art thou languid," first appeared in Dr. Neale's "Hymns of the Eastern Church," published in 1862. He gave it the quaint title, "Idiomela, in the Week of the First Oblique Tone." It is a translation from the Greek of St. Stephen the Sabaite, a monk who got his name from the monastery in which he lived, that of St. Sabas in the Kedron Valley, near Bethlehem, overlooking the Dead Sea. The monk, who was born in 725 A. D., was placed in that solitary monastery at the age of ten years by his uncle, and left there for fifty years. He died in 794. Here is the beautiful hymn that he wrote :—

Art thou weary, art thou languid,
　　Art thou sore distressed ?
" Come to me," saith One, " and, coming,
　　Be at rest."

Hath He marks to lead me to Him,
　　If He be my Guide ?
" In His feet and hands are wound-prints,
　　And His side."

Is there diadem as monarch,
　　That His brow adorns ?
" Yea, a crown, in very surety ;
　　But of thorns."

If I find Him, if I follow,
　　What His guerdon here ?
" Many a sorrow, many a labor,
　　Many a tear."

If I still hold closely to Him,
What hath He at last ?
" Sorrow vanquished, labor ended,
Jordan passed."

If I ask Him to receive me,
Will He say me nay?
" Not till earth and not till heaven
Pass away."

Finding, following, keeping, struggling,
Is He sure to bless ?
" Saints, apostles, prophets, martyrs,
Answer, Yes."

"Courage, Brother! Do Not Stumble!"

Norman Macleod

THIS is one of the most stirring and forcible hymns in the English language, vigorous in its expression, and full of fire and enthusiasm. It is the work of Rev. Norman Macleod, D. D., a Scottish clergyman, who was born at Campbeltown, June 3, 1812. His education was obtained in the universities of Glasgow and Edinburgh, and then in Germany. It was the University of Glasgow that gave him his degree of doctor of divinity.

Dr. Macleod was pastor of churches in Loudoun and Glasgow, and in 1841 he was made one of the chaplains to Queen Victoria. Among his notable achievements was the editing, from 1860 till his death, of the popular religious periodical, *Good Words*.

Dr. Macleod was a recognized leader in the Established Church of Scotland, and in 1869 became the moderator of its General Assembly. He died in Glasgow, June 20, 1872.

Dr. Macleod wrote many popular religious books in prose. The hymn before us is by far the best known of his poems. It appeared in January, 1857, in *The Edinburgh Christian Magazine*, which he edited for some years. The stirring stanzas are as follows : —

Courage, brother ! do not stumble,
  Though thy path be dark as night;
There's a star to guide the humble,
  Trust in God, and do the right.
Though the road be long and dreary,
  And the end be out of sight,
Tread it bravely, strong or weary,
  Trust in God, and do the right.

Perish policy and cunning,
  Perish all that fears the light,
Whether losing, whether winning,
  Trust in God, and do the right.
Shun all forms of guilty passion,
  Fiends can look like angels bright;
Heed no custom, school, or fashion,
  Trust in God, and do the right.

Some will hate thee, some will love thee,
  Some will flatter, some will slight;
Cease from man, and look above thee,
  Trust in God, and do the right.
Simple rule and safest guiding,
  Inward peace and shining light,
Star upon our path abiding,
  Trust in God, and do the right.

"Two Empires by the Sea"

George Huntington

THE International Hymn was written by George
Huntington, who was born November 5, 1835,
in Brooklyn, Conn., and who is now living in Northfield, Minn. Mr. Huntington is of good stock, as his
father was Dr. Thomas Huntington, and his grandfather was General Jedediah Huntington, of Norwich,
Conn., a Revolutionary officer.

After graduating at Brown University and taking
special studies in Andover Theological Seminary,
Mr. Huntington became pastor of several Congregational churches, and then professor of rhetoric and
Biblical literature in Carleton College, Northfield.
He has been editor of Sunday-school periodicals, has
contributed to various journals, and has written several volumes. He is now retired from his professor-
ship upon the Carnegie Foundation.

Professor Huntington's International Hymn was
written in 1896, at a time when there was some jingo
talk of war between Great Britain and the United
States, which was met by strong protests on the part
of all sensible people on both sides of the water.

The hymn was first published in *The Interior* of
Chicago (now *The Continent*), and was sung probably
for the first time in the Congregational church of
Northfield, Minn., on the Sunday following Wash-

ington's birthday, February 23, 1896, when the pastor, Rev. J. E. McConnell, preached a ringing sermon on conciliation, and President Strong offered a set of resolutions deprecating war and advocating a treaty of arbitration and an international court for the adjustment of international difficulties.

These resolutions were unanimously adopted by the congregation, and also by the other churches of the city to which copies had been sent, and the service closed with the singing of the International Hymn. The hymn was given to the Associated Press, and thus found its way into common use in the hymnals.

Mr. Andrew Carnegie used the hymn one year in the form of a New Year's card and distributed it extensively in the United States and Great Britain. International gatherings have used it not only in this country but in other lands, as in England, France, India, Japan, and New Zealand.

Professor Huntington writes me very modestly concerning his hymn, speaking of it as "a simple thing with no striking poetical quality, that has chanced to thrive upon popular sentiment. It was never intended as a rival or substitute for ' My Country, 'tis of Thee,' or as a national hymn, or as a universal peace hymn, but merely as the utterance of a sentiment of friendliness between England and our country." Such modesty is worthy of the author of this fine production.

When the hymn was written Queen Victoria was still upon the throne, and the third stanza in its closing lines read, "Great populace and Queen." The death of Queen Victoria made it necessary to change the hymn, which Professor Huntington has revised so that it reads as follows : —

Two empires by the sea,
Two nations great and free,
    One anthem raise.
One race of ancient fame,
One tongue, one faith, we claim,
One God, whose glorious name
    We love and praise.

What deeds our fathers wrought,
What battles we have fought,
    Let fame record.
Now, vengeful passion, cease ;
Come, victories of peace ;
Nor hate nor pride's caprice
    Unsheath the sword.

Though deep the sea, and wide,
'Twixt realm and realm, its tide
    Binds strand to strand.
So be the gulf between
Gray coasts and islands green
With bonds of peace serene,
    And friendship spanned.

Now may the God above
Guard the dear lands we love,
    Both East and West.
Let love more fervent glow,
As peaceful ages go,
And strength yet stronger grow,
    Blessing and blest.

"Summer Suns Are Glowing"
William Walsham How

A NUMBER of our best-known hymns were written by William Walsham How, who was born in Shrewsbury, England, December 13, 1823. He graduated from Oxford University in 1845, and at once entered the ministry of the Church of England. He became Dean and then Canon of Whittington, and in 1879 Queen Victoria made him Bishop of Bedford. In 1888 he became Bishop of Wakefield.

Bishop How was greatly beloved and honored. At one time in a public address he described the ideal minister, and all his hearers were impressed with the thought that he really presented a picture of his own life. "Such a minister," said Bishop How, "should be a man pure, holy, and spotless in his life; a man of much prayer; in character meek, lowly, and infinitely compassionate; of tenderest love to all; full of sympathy for every pain and sorrow, and devoting his days and nights to lightening the burdens of humanity; utterly patient of insult and enmity; utterly fearless in speaking the truth and rebuking sin; ever ready to answer every call, to go wherever bidden, in order to do good; wholly without thought of self; making himself the servant of all; patient, gentle, and untiring in dealing with the souls he would save; bearing with

ignorance, wilfulness, slowness, cowardice, in those
of whom he expects most; sacrificing all, even life
itself, if need be, to save some."

Bishop How wrote many books, including commentaries on the Gospels.   He was editor of several
collections of hymns, and contributed some original
hymns to these books.   In all he wrote about sixty
hymns.   These are simple, direct, musical, and
practical.   His best-known hymns are " O Jesus,
Thou art standing "; " For all the saints who from
their labors rest "; " We give Thee but Thine own ";
" O Word of God incarnate "; and " Jesus, name of
wondrous love."

Bishop How's summer hymn was published in
1871.   It was at first designed for children, but is
now used largely by their elders.   It is as follows:

> Summer suns are glowing
>   Over land and sea;
> Happy light is flowing
>   Bountiful and free.
> Everything rejoices
>   In the mellow rays;
> All earth's thousand voices
>   Swell the psalm of praise.
>
> God's free mercy streameth
>   Over all the world,
> And His banner gleameth
>   Everywhere unfurled.
> Broad and deep and glorious
>   As the heaven above,
> Shines in might victorious
>   His eternal love.

Lord, upon our blindness,
   Thy pure radiance pour;
For Thy loving-kindness
   Makes us love Thee more.
And when clouds are drifting
   Dark across our sky,
Then, the veil uplifting,
   Father, be Thou nigh.

We will never doubt Thee,
   Though Thou veil Thy light;
Life is dark without Thee;
   Death with Thee is bright.
Light of light! shine o'er us
   On our pilgrim way;
Go Thou still before us
   To the endless day.

"Behold! a Stranger at the Door"
Joseph Grigg

THIS beautiful hymn, a prime favorite with old and young, was written by an Englishman, Joseph Grigg. The date of his birth is uncertain, but it was probably 1720. His parents were poor, and he was raised as a mechanic. In 1743, however, he became an assistant minister in a London Presbyterian church. Upon his marriage to a wealthy widow in 1747 he retired from his pastorate, though he continued to preach frequently in the pulpits of his brother ministers. He died on October 29, 1768.

Mr. Grigg wrote more than forty books, and about forty hymns. It is said that he began to write hymns when he was ten years old, and the hymn before us is probably among the number of those written at that early age. At any rate, it appeared in the *Gospel Magazine* for April, 1774, with the title, "'Shame of Jesus Conquered by Love,' by a youth of ten years." That would make the date of the hymn 1730. Only one other of Mr. Grigg's hymns is of equal popularity, "Jesus, and can it ever be?"

The five stanzas of our hymn are as follows:—

Behold! a Stranger at the door;
He gently knocks, has knocked before;
Has waited long, is waiting still;
You treat no other friend so ill.

Oh, lovely attitude ! He stands
With melting heart and laden hands ;
Oh, matchless kindness ! and He shows
This matchless kindness to His foes.

But will He prove a friend indeed ?
He will, the very friend you need —
The Friend of sinners ; yes, 'tis He,
With garments dyed on Calvary.

Rise, touched with gratitude divine ;
Turn out His enemy and thine,
That soul-destroying monster, sin,
And let the heavenly Stranger in.

Admit Him ere His anger burn ;
His feet, departed, ne'er return ;
Admit Him, or the hour 's at hand
When at His door denied you'll stand.

"Bright Was the Guiding Star That Led"
Harriet Auber

HARRIET AUBER was born in London, October 4, 1773. She led a quiet, secluded life, greatly beloved by all her many friends. She was a member of the Church of England. In 1829 she published a book, "The Spirit of the Psalms," which was a collection of poems based upon the Psalms. Many of the best poems in this volume were from her own pen.

Though she wrote many poems, she is known chiefly for her Christmas hymn, and for the very beautiful hymn, "Our blest Redeemer, ere He breathed," etc. Among her other hymns that are in common use are, "Sweet is the work, O Lord," "With joy we hail the sacred day," "Wide, ye heavenly gates, unfold," and the splendid missionary hymn based on Psalm 72, "Hasten, Lord! the glorious time." Her Christmas hymn is as follows:

Bright was the guiding star that led,
　With mild, benignant ray,
The Gentiles to the lowly shed,
　Where the Redeemer lay.

But, lo! a brighter, clearer light
　Now points to His abode;
It shines, through sin and sorrow's night,
　To guide us to our God.

Oh ! haste to follow where it leads,
  The gracious call obey ;
Be rugged wilds, or flowery meads,
  The Christian's destined way.

Oh ! gladly tread the narrow path,
  While light and grace are given ;
Who meekly follow Christ on earth
  Shall reign with Him in heaven.

" Father, Let Me Dedicate "
Lawrence Tuttiett

THE author of this New Year's hymn, Lawrence Tuttiett, was the son of John Tuttiett, a surgeon of the Royal Navy of England. He was born in Cloyton, in Devonshire, 1825, and was educated at King's College, London. It was the intention to make him a physician, but he chose the ministry, and in 1848 became a clergyman of the Church of England. His parishes were first in Warwickshire and then in Scotland.

Mr. Tuttiett wrote several volumes of hymns. His hymns are smooth, straightforward, simple, and earnest. Especially valuable are those that deal with special services of the church and with special seasons of the year, like the New Year's hymn we are to commit to memory. Among his best-known hymns are, " Grant us Thy light, that we may know," " O quickly come, dread Judge of all," " O happy Christian child," and " Go forward, Christian soldier." " Father, let me dedicate," which is probably the favorite among all his hymns, was written in 1864, and is as follows:—

> Father, let me dedicate
> All this year to Thee,
> In whatever worldly state
> Thou wilt have me be.

137

Not from sorrow, pain, or care,
   Freedom dare I claim ;
This alone shall be my prayer :
   Glorify Thy name.

Can a child presume to choose
   Where or how to live ?
Can a Father's love refuse
   All the best to give ?
More Thou givest every day
   Than the best can claim,
Nor withholdest aught that may
   Glorify Thy name.

If in mercy Thou wilt spare
   Joys that yet are mine ;
If on life, serene and fair,
   Brighter rays may shine,—
Let my glad heart, while it sings,
   Thee in all proclaim,
And whate'er the future brings,
   Glorify Thy name.

If Thou callest to the cross,
   And its shadow come,
Turning all my gain to loss,
   Shrouding heart and home,—
Let me think how Thy dear Son
   To His glory came,
And in deepest woe pray on,
   " Glorify Thy name."

"Oh, Could I Speak the Matchless Worth"
Samuel Medley

SAMUEL MEDLEY was born in Cheshunt, England, June 23, 1738. His father was a schoolteacher, and the lad received a good education and was then apprenticed to an oil-merchant in London. He did not like the business, however, and took advantage of a law which allowed an apprentice, if he chose, to complete his term of apprenticeship by serving in the navy.

Medley, therefore, became a midshipman in 1755, which was during the Seven Years' War. In 1759 he was severely wounded in a battle with the French off Port Lagos. He had been brought up to have a high regard for religion, but in the navy he had become dissipated. As he lay there wounded and expecting that amputation of a limb would be necessary, he spent nearly an entire night in prayers of penitence, and in the morning the surgeon, surprised at his improved condition, told him that the limb could be saved.

He was taken for recovery to the house of his grandfather in London, and the pious old man labored earnestly for his conversion. At last the light came to him as his grandfather read to him a sermon by Dr. Watts on Isa. 42 : 6, 7. He left the navy, married, and taught school for four years. Then he was induced to begin preaching, and at last, in 1767, he became pastor of a Baptist church. For twenty-seven years he was pastor of a large church in Liverpool, where he was especially successful in reaching sailors, since he never forgot that he had been a sailor himself, and filled his sermons with expressions that reached the men of the sea. Indeed, as Medley lay on his death-bed his last words were such as a sailor might speak: "I am now a poor shattered bark, just about to gain the blissful harbor, and oh, how sweet will be the port after the storm! But a point or two more and I shall be at my heavenly Father's house!" His death occurred July 17, 1799.

Medley wrote many hymns, most of which were printed on broadsides, or loose sheets of paper, and several volumes of his hymns appeared. Among the most famous are "Father of mercies, God of love," "Jesus, engrave it on my heart," "Awake, my soul, to joyful lays," and the hymn which is probably the favorite among all his hymns, "Oh, could I speak the matchless worth." The following is the hymn :—

> Oh, could I speak the matchless worth,
> Oh, could I sound the glories forth,
>   Which in my Saviour shine,
> I'd soar, and touch the heavenly strings,
> And vie with Gabriel while he sings
>   In notes almost divine.

I'd sing the precious blood He spilt,
My ransom from the dreadful guilt
    Of sin, and wrath divine;
I'd sing His glorious righteousness,
In which all-perfect, heavenly dress
    My soul shall ever shine.

I'd sing the characters He bears,
And all the forms of love He wears,
    Exalted on His throne;
In loftiest songs of sweetest praise
I would to everlasting days
    Make all His glories known.

Well, the delightful day will come
When my dear Lord will bring me home,
    And I shall see His face;
Then with my Saviour, Brother, Friend,
A blest eternity I'll spend,
    Triumphant in His grace.

"Crown Him with Many Crowns"
Matthew Bridges

MATTHEW BRIDGES, who wrote this famous hymn, is one of a number of Roman Catholics whose beautiful hymns have become favorites with Protestant worshippers of all denominations. He was at first, however, a member of the Church of England.

Born in Maldon, Essex, England, July 14, 1800, he began to publish verses in 1825, and continued until several volumes of poems had appeared, with some work in prose. Most of his hymns that have obtained popularity are to be found in his "Hymns of the Heart," which was published in 1848, the year he became a Catholic. He afterward moved to the Province of Quebec, and passed from earth on October 6, 1894.

Mr. Bridges's hymns are marked by spirituality and genuine power. Among the best known are "Lo, He comes with clouds descending," "My God, accept my heart this day," and "Behold, the Lamb of God."

Undoubtedly his greatest hymn is "Crown Him with many crowns." It first appeared in his book, "The Passion of Jesus," published in 1852. The title given it in that book is "The Song of the Seraphs." This is the hymn :—

Crown Him with many crowns,
    The Lamb upon His throne;
Hark! how the heavenly anthem drowns
    All music but its own.
Awake, my soul, and sing
    Of Him who died for thee,
And hail Him as thy matchless King
    Through all eternity.

Crown Him the Lord of love;
    Behold His hands and side,
Rich wounds, yet visible above
    In beauty glorified.
No angel in the sky
    Can fully bear that sight,
But downward bends his wondering eye
    At mysteries so bright.

Crown Him the Lord of peace,
    Whose power a sceptre sways
From pole to pole, that wars may cease,
    And all be prayer and praise.
His reign shall know no end.
    And round His piercèd feet
Fair flowers of paradise extend
    Their fragrance ever sweet.

Crown Him the Lord of years,
    The potentate of time,
Creator of the rolling spheres,
    Ineffably sublime.
All hail, Redeemer, hail!
    For Thou hast died for me;
Thy praise shall never, never fail
    Throughout eternity.

" O Love That Wilt Not Let Me Go "
George Matheson

GEORGE MATHESON was one of the most re-markable men that have ever lived, on account of the great work he did in spite of the terrible handicap of blindness.

He was born in Glasgow, Scotland, March 27, 1842. When a boy he had partial vision, but his eyesight gradually failed, and all through his course in Glasgow University, and from his graduation on, he was entirely dependent upon others. He was, however, never totally blind, but he had moments of shadowy eyesight.

This affliction was a terrible tragedy, as he was an eager and ambitious scholar ; but it threw him back upon God, and undoubtedly deepened his spiritual life. His two sisters were devoted to him, and even learned Latin, Greek, and Hebrew that they might help him in his studies.

Entering the university at the age of fifteen, he graduated with distinction in 1861, afterward spending four more years in his theological studies.

Almost immediately upon completing his theological course he became assistant pastor to the famous Dr. Macduff, in whose church of thousands of members he had been brought up. Soon, however, he was chosen minister of the Church of Scotland in the seaport summer resort of Innellan. Here he remained for eighteen years, and many families came to spend the summer there chiefly because of his pulpit ministrations.

At this time he was in the habit of committing his sermons to memory, as he committed to memory the passages of the Bible that were used in the pulpit. The open Bible was before him, and he seemed to be reading from it. His eyes during the sermon looked straight at the audience, and many went away with no idea that they had been listening to a blind preacher.

His memory was so retentive that after listening to two readings of his sermon, or whatever he was committing to memory, he could repeat it perfectly. One Sunday, however, after twelve years of this practice, when he was in the midst of an eloquent sermon, his memory suffered a complete collapse, the sermon passing entirely out of his mind. He gave out a Psalm, seated himself, and on the conclusion of the singing, with perfect self-possession, told the audience what had happened, gave out a new text, and preached an extempore sermon of great power. From that time he wrote comparatively little of his sermons, and finally prepared only an outline from which he preached.

Dr. Matheson's second and concluding pastorate was taken up in 1886, when he became minister of the large St. Bernard's Church in Edinburgh. Here he remained for thirteen years, great crowds coming to hear him, and his church grew during the first five years from 1,494 to 1,703 communicants.

During all his ministerial work Dr. Matheson was a most faithful pastor as well as a great preacher, and was most assiduous in making pastoral calls. In all of this work he was wonderfully aided by his faithful sister, who lived with him.

He spent the concluding years of his life in literary labors, preaching only on special occasions, and passed away on August 28, 1906, after completing an amount of varied and distinguished work which would have taxed the resources of any man having complete vision.

Dr. Matheson wrote many books, all of them characterized by deep spiritual insight and mental vigor. Among these the most remarkable were his various books on Bible characters and on Christ, and his devotional books, beginning with "Moments on the Mount."

Of his hymns, the one before us is by far the most famous. It was written at Innellan, when he was alone in the manse, on the evening of June 6, 1882. At that time he was enduring much mental suffering, and the hymn was the beautiful product of it.

It was a genuine inspiration. He called it "the quickest bit of work I ever did in my life." It was all written out in five minutes, and he made no corrections or changes in it afterward. The appropriate and striking tune written for it was produced by the composer at the same rate of speed.

Here is the hymn :—

> O Love that wilt not let me go,
>   I rest my weary soul in Thee :
> I give Thee back the life I owe,
> That in Thine ocean depths its flow
>   May richer, fuller be.

O Light that followest all my way,
    I yield my flickering torch to Thee :
My heart restores its borrowed ray,
That in Thy sunshine's blaze its day
    May brighter, fairer be.

O Joy that seekest me through pain,
    I cannot close my heart to Thee :
I trace the rainbow through the rain,
And feel the promise is not vain
    That morn shall tearless be.

O Cross that liftest up my head,
    I dare not ask to fly from Thee :
I lay in dust life's glory dead,
And from the ground there blossoms red
    Life that shall endless be.

"Jesus, the Very Thought of Thee"
Bernard of Clairvaux

THE most famous hymn of the Middle Ages was a Latin hymn written by Bernard of Clairvaux, and this hymn is an English translation of a portion of that Latin hymn.

Bernard was the son of a French knight, and was born in his father's castle near Dijon in Burgundy, in the year 1091. He was a studious lad, beautiful in face and form, and graceful in manners. The rank of his family opened before him a career of power. He was led, however, partly by a dream of his mother's, to become a monk.

This plan was carried out in 1113, and he won his uncle and two of his brothers to enter the monastery with him. In two years so great was the influence he gained that he was sent forth to found a new monastery, and was known from that time as the Abbot of Clairvaux.

On the death of the Pope, Honorius II., in 1830, two rival Popes disputed the throne, and the French clergy left it to Bernard to decide which Pope France should follow. Bernard's decision was for Innocent II., and the Abbot of Clairvaux won to his side Henry I. of England, and Lothair, the Emperor of Germany. Innocent II., though unsuccessful at first, finally became the sole Pope, and Bernard of course was very powerful at his court.

In 1146 Bernard preached the second crusade, and with great eloquence enlisted in this luckless enterprise the religious people of France and Germany. A vast horde set forth in 1147, but not a tenth of them ever reached Palestine. Those that gained that goal were easily defeated, and the expedition failed miserably. Bernard was blamed for its failure, and died not long afterward, in 1153, at the age of sixty-three—a weary and disappointed man.

The Latin hymns attributed to Bernard are not known positively to be his, but certainly to no one else could hymns of so great beauty and power be attributed, and they coincide in many of their expressions and thoughts with Bernard's acknowledged work in prose.

The best of his hymns, "*Jesu Dulcis Memoria*," often called "The Name of Jesus," was written possibly in 1150, during Bernard's retirement after the crusade. The hymn consists of forty-two stanzas of four lines each, and is a worthy product of the *Doctor Mellifluous*, or "Honeyed Teacher," which was Bernard's popular name.

The Latin hymn has become a mine for beautiful translations. Perhaps the best is that by Edward Caswall, a Catholic clergyman of England, and the most popular translator of the Latin hymns with the exception of J. M. Neale. I have chosen the most famous portion of the great hymn. It was translated by Caswall in 1848, and is as follows :—

Jesus, the very thought of Thee
   With sweetness fills my breast;
But sweeter far Thy face to see,
   And in Thy presence rest.

Nor voice can sing, nor heart can frame,
   Nor can the memory find
A sweeter sound than Thy blest name,
   O Saviour of mankind.

O hope of every contrite heart,
   O joy of all the meek.
To those who fall, how kind Thou art;
   How good to those who seek !

But what to those who find?   Ah, this
   Nor tongue nor pen can show;
The love of Jesus, what it is,
   None but His loved ones know.

Jesus, our only joy be Thou,
   As Thou our prize shalt be;
Jesus, be Thou our glory now,
   And through eternity.

"Majestic Sweetness Sits Enthroned"
Samuel Stennett

THIS great hymn was written by Samuel Stennett, who was born in Exeter, England, probably in the year 1727. His father, a Baptist minister, moved to London while Samuel was a boy. In 1748 his son became his assistant, and in 1758 Stennett succeeded his father in the pastorate of the London church, a position which he held for the remainder of his life.

He became a very prominent minister, greatly honored by British statesmen, and was able by means of this influence to moderate the intolerance with which Baptists were regarded in those days. King George III. was among his friends. He consistently refused the promotion which was well within his reach, though he did accept the degree of doctor of divinity, which was given him in 1763 from the University of Aberdeen.

Among his famous friends was John Howard, the great prison reformer, who was a member of his congregation. Howard wrote from Smyrna at one time telling of his pleasure in often reviewing his notes of Dr. Stennett's sermons. Stennett died on August 24, 1795.

Besides several volumes of sermons, Dr. Stennett wrote thirty-eight hymns. Most of these were con-

tributed to Rippon's famous collection, which was
published in 1787. Among Stennett's hymns that
are often sung are the following: "Come, every
pious heart," "How charming is the place," "'Tis
finished! so the Saviour cried," and "On Jordan's
stormy banks I stand." His greatest hymn, however, is the following, which was first published in
1787, as a hymn of nine stanzas (now condensed to
six), with the title, "Chief among Ten Thousand;
or, the Excellencies of Christ," and with the Scripture reference, Solomon's Song 5 : 10–16 :—

> Majestic sweetness sits enthroned
>   Upon the Saviour's brow;
> His head with radiant glories crowned,
>   His lips with grace o'erflow.
>
> No mortal can with Him compare
>   Among the sons of men;
> Fairer is He than all the fair
>   That fill the heavenly train.
>
> He saw me plunged in deep distress,
>   He flew to my relief;
> For me He bore the shameful cross,
>   And carried all my grief.
>
> To Him I owe my life and breath,
>   And all the joys I have;
> He makes me triumph over death,
>   He saves me from the grave.
>
> To heaven, the place of His abode,
>   He brings my weary feet;
> Shows me the glories of my God,
>   And makes my joy complete.

Since from His bounty I receive
Such proofs of love divine,
Had I a thousand hearts to give,
Lord, they should all be Thine.

"The Battle Hymn of the Republic"
Julia Ward Howe

THIS great song by Julia Ward Howe did much to inspire the Union army during the Civil War.

The author was born on May 27, 1819, in Bowling Green, at the lower part of New York City. She was a brilliant girl, and as early as seventeen began to write for the leading magazines of the country. At the age of twenty-four she married Dr. Samuel Gridley Howe of Boston, the head of Perkins Institute, the Massachusetts School for the Blind. Charles Dickens had just made him famous by a glowing account of the wonderful work he had done with the deaf, dumb, and blind Laura Bridgman. Dr. Howe was also an enthusiast for Grecian liberty and accomplished much for that nation, then in its war for freedom.

All of Mrs. Howe's children are literary workers. Her son is a professor in Columbia University. Her three daughters that are now living, Laura E. Richards, Florence Howe Hall, and Maud Howe Elliott, are well-known writers. Mrs. Howe herself wrote four volumes of poems, and several volumes of essays, biographies, and travel. She was the most honored woman in Boston, and probably the most honored woman in America.

Up to her death, in 1910, at the notable age of ninety-one, she retained remarkable vigor. Her brilliant services were often in demand on public occasions. She still presided over the Boston Authors' Club and the New England Women's Club. Much of her continued strength and intellectual clearness she attributed to her habit of daily study. It was a great inspiration to hear her recite, as I have heard her more than once, the splendid stanzas of " The Battle Hymn of the Republic."

This song was written in 1861, after she had visited the camp of the Union army on the Potomac. The soldiers had been marching by her, singing the rough popular song, "John Brown's Body." As they passed she had spoken to them, expressing the wish that she might some time write words for the magnificent swinging melody of their song. She returned to her lodgings in Washington, worn by the long, cold drive, and slept soundly; but she awoke before daybreak with her song in her mind, and wrote the stanzas in the dark, then returning to sleep.

Here are the five stanzas of the hymn, though in most of our hymn-books the third stanza is omitted :—

Mine eyes have seen the glory of the coming of the Lord;
He is trampling out the vintage where the grapes of wrath are
    stored;
He hath loosed the fateful lightning of His terrible swift
    sword;
      His truth is marching on.

I have seen Him in the watch-fires of a hundred circling camps,
They have builded Him an altar in the evening dews and
    damps;
I can read His righteous sentence by the dim and flaring
    lamps;
      His day is marching on.

I have read a fiery gospel writ in burnished rows of steel;
" As ye deal with my contemners, so with you my grace shall
    deal ";
Let the Hero, born of woman, crush the serpent with His heel,
      Since God is marching on.

He hath sounded forth the trumpet that shall never call
    retreat;
He is sifting out the hearts of men before His judgment seat;
Oh, be swift, my soul, to answer Him! be jubilant, my feet!
      Our God is marching on.

In the beauty of the lilies Christ was born across the sea,
With a glory in His bosom that transfigures you and me;
As He died to make men holy, let us die to make men free,
      While God is marching on.

" For the Beauty of the Earth "
Folliott Sandford Pierpoint

THIS beautiful summer hymn, full of the spirit of field and forest, was written by Folliott Sandford Pierpoint, about whose life I can learn little. He was born in Bath, England, October 7, 1835, and obtained his education at Queen's College in Cambridge University, graduating with classical honors in 1871. He published several volumes of poems, but his work is best known by this hymn, which appeared in 1864. It has been changed in many lines, but the following is perhaps the best version :—

> For the beauty of the earth,
>   For the beauty of the skies,
> For the love which from our birth
>   Over and around us lies :
> Christ, our God, to Thee we raise
> This, our sacrifice of praise.
>
> For the beauty of each hour
>   Of the day and of the night,
> Hill and vale, and tree and flower,
>   Sun and moon and stars of light :
> Christ, our God, to Thee we raise
> This, our sacrifice of praise.
>
> For the joy of human love,
>   Brother, sister, parent, child,
> Friends on earth, and friends above ;
>   For all gentle thoughts and mild :
> Christ, our God, to Thee we raise
> This, our sacrifice of praise.

For each perfect gift of Thine
　To our race so freely given,
Graces, human and divine,
　Flowers of earth, and buds of heaven :
Christ, our God, to Thee we raise
This, our sacrifice of praise.

For Thy church that evermore
　Lifteth holy hands above,
Offering up on every shore
　Its pure sacrifice of love :
Christ, our God, to Thee we raise
This, our sacrifice of praise.

"Onward, Christian, Though the Region"
Samuel Johnson

SAMUEL JOHNSON, who wrote this hymn, was not the famous English essayist and dictionary-maker, but was an American clergyman, who was born in Salem, Mass., October 10, 1822. After graduating from Harvard he became pastor of an undenominational church in Lynn, Mass., in 1853, and remained its pastor till 1870. He was usually associated with the Unitarians.

Mr. Johnson was a man of much learning, and wrote a very able book on "Oriental Religions." He edited with Samuel Longfellow, brother of Henry Wadsworth Longfellow, in 1846, "A Book of Hymns," to which he contributed the hymn we are studying, and also another very beautiful hymn, "Father, in Thy mysterious presence kneeling." He was also editor, with Mr. Longfellow, of "Hymns of the Spirit," for which he wrote a hymn that has come into common use, "City of God, how broad and fair." Mr. Johnson died at North Andover, February 19, 1882.

The original title for our hymn was "Conflict," and its stanzas are as follows : —

> Onward, Christian, though the region
> Where thou art be drear and lone ;
> God has set a guardian legion
> Very near thee ; press thou on.

By the thorn-road, and none other,
    Is the mount of vision won :
Tread it without shrinking, brother —
    Jesus trod it ; press thou on.

Be this world the wiser, stronger,
    For thy life of pain and peace ;
While it needs thee, oh ! no longer
    Pray thou for thy quick release.

Pray thou, Christian, daily rather
    That thou be a faithful son ;
By the prayer of Jesus, " Father,
    Not my will, but Thine, be done."

"O Golden Day So Long Desired"
Charles Albert Dickinson

THE author of this hymn was one of the best-beloved and most influential of Christian Endeavor leaders, Rev. Charles Albert Dickinson, D. D. He was born in Westminster, Vt., July 4, 1849. As a part of his wide-spread Christian work he afterward made his birthplace the nucleus of a useful home for boys and girls, which is in successful operation to-day.

He graduated in 1872 from Phillips Academy, Andover, and went to Harvard University, from which he graduated in 1876, being the class poet. In 1879 he graduated from Andover Theological Seminary, and was married on July 2 of the same year. At once he became pastor of the Payson Memorial Church, Portland, Me., the church made famous by the revered Edward Payson. He was deeply interested in the progress of the first Christian Endeavor society in the neighboring Williston Church, and was one of the very earliest friends of the cause, perhaps the first, to join Dr. Clark in bringing Christian Endeavor to the attention of other ministers.

In 1882 Dr. Dickinson became pastor of the Kirk Street Congregational Church of Lowell, Mass., and

in 1888 took up his great work in Berkeley Temple,
Boston. He built up this church along institutional lines and made it a great hive of Christian
industry of all kinds. Dr. Dickinson was the
first exponent of institutional church work in America. He believed in it heartily, and got many
others to believe in it and to follow his enthusiastic
example.

Failing health sent Dr. Dickinson to California,
where he served as pastor of the First Congregational Church of Sacramento for two years. He
died on January 9, 1907.

Dr. Dickinson was a most lovable man, full of
good cheer and friendliness. He was deeply interested in Christian Endeavor from the start. He
always attended the International Conventions, and
he presided over the Convention at Cleveland, from
which Dr. Clark was obliged to be absent on account of sickness.

In company with Dr. Clark, Dr. Dickinson made
a memorable visit to Great Britain, speaking in the
interests of Christian Endeavor, and it was upon his
return from this visit, in June, 1891, that he wrote
the hymn we are to commit to memory. The ship
had for four days been in the grasp of a terrific
storm. When the storm ceased, out of the thankfulness of his heart Dr. Dickinson wrote this hymn,
which has new interest and meaning when we remember its origin.

The hymn is one of great beauty. It was sung
at the Boston service in memory of Dr. Dickinson
on May 12, 1907. It is one of the favorite hymns

of British Endeavorers, and not long before his death Dr. Dickinson received a letter from that leader of musical interests among British Endeavorers, Rev. Carey Bonner of London, the secretary of the British Sunday-School Union.   Mr. Bonner says in this letter :

"I do not know whether you are aware of the great hold which your hymn, 'O golden day,' has taken upon British Endeavorers.   We inserted it in our Christian Endeavor hymnal, and at once, in the early convention days, it became a favorite, and now there are no verses more acceptable and more popular than those you penned. Again and again I have heard great masses of young people sing your hymn with tremendous enthusiasm and power. The words embody not only a central belief of Christian Endeavor, but a great truth for the church at large, a truth which happily Christ's men and women are more and more appreciating and seeking to carry out."

The hymn, which is one of the finest expressions of that sentiment for Christian union which Christian Endeavor has done so much to promote, is as follows :—

> O golden day so long desired,
>   Born of a darksome night,
> The swinging globe at last is fired
>   By thy resplendent light.
> And hark! like Memnon's morning chord
>   Is heard from sea to sea
> This song : One Master, Christ, the Lord ;
>   And brethren all are we.

The noises of the night shall cease,
  The storms no longer roar ;
The factious foes of God's own peace
  Shall vex His church no more.
A thousand thousand voices sing
  In surging harmony
This song : One Master, Saviour, King ;
  And brethren all are we.

Sing on, ye chorus of the morn,
  Your grand Endeavor strain,
Till Christian hearts, estranged and torn,
  Blend in the glad refrain ;
And all the church, with all its pow'rs,
  In loving loyalty
Shall sing : One Master, Christ, is ours ;
  And brethren all are we.

" In the Field with Their Flocks "
Frederic William Farrar

THIS beautiful Christmas hymn was written by a very famous man, Frederic William Farrar, who was born in Bombay, India, August 7, 1831. His father was at that time a missionary to India, and afterward he became rector of a church in England.

Young Farrar had the unique experience of graduating from two colleges, first from King's College, London, and then from Trinity College, Cambridge, obtaining distinguished honors in both of these courses.

He became a clergyman of the Church of England, but the earlier portion of his career was as an educator. He was assistant master of Harrow School, and then head master of Marlborough College.

When he entered definitely upon his ministerial work his advancement was rapid. First he became Canon of Westminster Abbey, then Archdeacon in 1883, and finally, in 1895, he was made Dean of Canterbury. He served as preacher before the University of Cambridge, as chaplain to the speaker of the House of Commons, and as chaplain to Queen Victoria.

Dean Farrar was a most brilliant and inspiring preacher. He was at the same time one of the greatest writers of his day, treating with a most unusual

vividness and charm a great variety of topics. He
wrote many books, the best-known being a life of
Christ, a life of Paul, "Seekers after God," and
"Christ in Art." He also wrote a number of stirring
stories for boys, and some books upon temperance,
of which cause he was an ardent advocate. He died
at the age of seventy-one, on March 22, 1903.

Dean Farrar's hymns are few, but they are very
beautiful, and perhaps the finest of them all is this
Christmas hymn. It is as follows : —

> In the fields with their flocks abiding,
>   They lay on the dewy ground ;
> And glimmering under the starlight
>   The sheep lay white around,
> When the light of the Lord streamed o'er them,
>   And lo ! from the heaven above,
> An angel leaned from the glory
>   And sang his song of love :
> He sang, that first sweet Christmas,
>   The song that shall never cease,
> " Glory to God in the highest,
>   On earth good will and peace.

> " To you in the City of David
>   A Saviour is born to-day ! "
> And sudden a host of the heavenly ones
>   Flashed forth to join the lay !
> O never hath sweeter message
>   Thrilled home to the souls of men,
> And the heavens themselves had never heard
>   A gladder choir till then,
> For they sang that Christmas carol
>   That never on earth shall cease :
> " Glory to God in the highest,
>   On earth good will and peace."

And the shepherds came to the manger,
  And gazed on the Holy Child ;
And calmly o'er that rude cradle
  The Virgin Mother smiled ;
And the sky in the star-lit silence
  Seemed full of the angel lay :
" To you in the City of David
  A Saviour is born to-day."
  O, they sang—and I ween that never
  The carol on earth shall cease :
" Glory to God in the highest,
  On earth good will and peace."

"Rise, My Soul, and Stretch Thy Wings"
Robert Seagrave

THIS hymn was written by Rev. Robert Seagrave, about whom not many facts have come down to us. He was born in Twyford, Leicestershire, England, November 22, 1693. He obtained his education at Cambridge University, became a clergyman of the Church of England, and grew much interested in the work of the Wesleys and of Whitefield. From 1739 to 1750 he was Sunday-evening lecturer at Loriner's Hall, London. He often preached in Whitefield's tabernacle. His hymns were collected in 1742, this among them. It is the only one of them all that is now in common use, but it is a very beautiful and stirring Christian song. It has three double stanzas, running as follows : —

Rise, my soul, and stretch thy wings,
 Thy better portion trace ;
Rise from transitory things
 Toward heaven, thy native place :
Sun and moon and stars decay ;
 Time shall soon this earth remove ;
Rise, my soul, and haste away
 To seats prepared above.

Rivers to the ocean run,
 Nor stay in all their course ;
Fire ascending seeks the sun ;
 Both speed them to their source :

So a soul that's born of God
   Pants to view His glorious face ;
Upward tends to His abode,
   To rest in His embrace.

Cease, ye pilgrims, cease to mourn ;
   Press onward to the prize ;
Soon our Saviour will return
   Triumphant in the skies ;
Yet a season—and you know
   Happy entrance will be given,
All our sorrows left below,
   And earth exchanged for heaven.

" Sweet Hour of Prayer "
William W. Walford

NOT much is known about the writer of this favorite gospel hymn. He was a blind man, Rev. William W. Walford, an English clergyman. It is quite remarkable how many of our best hymns have been written by blind people who themselves sang "songs in the night." Fanny Crosby and George Matheson occur to us at once.

Mr. Walford preached, but not regularly, and he had a pair of skilful hands that made various little things of bone and ivory. He wrote our hymn probably about the year 1842, and recited it to Rev. Thomas Salmon, a Congregational minister of Coleshill, England, who wrote it down and brought it to New York, where it was published in *The New York Observer*. This seems to be all that is known about the hymn or its author.

Very few Christians know by heart the whole of this hymn, but it is all worth committing to memory. Mr. Walford's life must have been full of trouble, and we find references to it in the hymn ; but we see also how his religion lifted him above his trouble. It will do the same for us.

> Sweet hour of prayer ! sweet hour of prayer !
> That calls me from a world of care,
> And bids me at my Father's throne
> Make all my wants and wishes known :

In seasons of distress and grief
My soul has often found relief,
And oft escaped the tempter's snare,
By thy return, sweet hour of prayer !

Sweet hour of prayer ! sweet hour of prayer !
Thy wings shall my petition bear
To Him whose truth and faithfulness
Engage the waiting soul to bless :
And since He bids me seek His face,
Believe His word, and trust His grace,
I'll cast on Him my every care,
And wait for thee, sweet hour of prayer !

Sweet hour of prayer ! sweet hour of prayer
May I thy consolation share,
Till, from Mount Pisgah's lofty height,
I view my home and take my flight ;
This robe of flesh I'll drop, and rise
To seize the everlasting prize ;
And shout, while passing through the air,
Farewell, farewell, sweet hour of prayer !

"The Day of Resurrection"

St. John of Damascus

ST. JOHN of Damascus was next to the last of the series of great religious leaders belonging to the Eastern or Greek Catholic Church. He was the greatest of the poets produced by that church. The Arabs called him Ibn Mansur, which probably means "Son of a Conqueror."

He was born in Damascus early in the eighth century, and held some office under the Caliph. Late in life he resigned this office, became a priest of the Jerusalem church, and ended his life in a convent near Jerusalem—the convent of St. Sabas. He died about A. D. 780, either in his eighty-fourth or in his one-hundredth year.

St. John of Damascus wrote important prose works on theology, and many great poems from which the Greek Church has taken some of its best-loved hymns. He was particularly fond of writing about the birth and the resurrection of Christ. John Mason Neale, who translated so finely many of the great Greek and Latin hymns, has translated two written by St. John of Damascus—"Come, ye faithful, raise the strain," and the hymn before us. His translation—which is only a part of a much longer poem—is as follows :—

The day of resurrection,
   Earth, tell it out abroad :
The Passover of gladness,
   The Passover of God.
From death to life eternal,
   From earth unto the sky,
Our Christ hath brought us over
   With hymns of victory.

Our hearts be pure from evil,
   That we may see aright
The Lord in rays eternal
   Of resurrection light ;
And, listening to His accents,
   May hear, so calm and plain,
His own " All hail ! " and, hearing,
   May raise the victor-strain.

Now let the heavens be joyful,
   And earth her song begin,
The round world keep high triumph,
   And all that is therein ;
Let all things seen and unseen
   Their notes of gladness blend,
For Christ the Lord is risen,
   Our Joy that hath no end.

Dr. Neale admired this hymn greatly, and he
wrote the following vivid account of the way in
which it used to be sung by Greek Christians :

"As midnight approached, the archbishop, with
his priests, accompanied by the king and queen, left
the church and stationed themselves on the platform,
which was raised considerably from the ground, so
that they were distinctly seen by the people.   Every
one now remained in breathless expectation, holding

an unlighted taper in readiness when the glad moment should arrive, while the priests still continued
murmuring their melancholy chant in a low half
whisper.   Suddenly a single report of a cannon announced that twelve o'clock had struck and that
Easter Day had begun; then the old archbishop,
elevating the cross, exclaimed in a loud, exulting
tone, ' *Christos aneste !* '   ' Christ is risen !' and instantly every single individual of all that host took
up the cry, and the vast multitude broke through
and dispelled forever the intense and mournful
silence which they had maintained so long with one
spontaneous shout of indescribable joy and triumph,
'Christ is risen!'   'Christ is risen!'   At the same
moment the oppressive darkness was succeeded by
a blaze of light from thousands of tapers which, com-
municating to one from another, seemed to send
streams of fire in all directions, rendering the minut-
est objects distinctly visible, and casting the most
vivid glow on the expressive faces, full of exultation,
of the rejoicing crowd; bands of music struck up
their gayest strains; the roll of a drum through the
town, and further on the pealing of the cannon, announced far and near these 'glad tidings of great
joy'; while from hill and plain, from the seashore
and the far olive grove, rocket after rocket, ascending to the clear sky, answered back with its mute
eloquence that Christ is risen indeed, and told of
other tongues that were repeating those blessed
words, and other hearts that leaped for joy ; everywhere men clasped each other's hands, and con-
gratulated one another and embraced with counte-

nances beaming with delight, as though to each one separately some wonderful happiness had been proclaimed ; and so, in truth, it was ; and all the while, rising above the mingling of many sounds, each one of which was a sound of gladness, the aged priests were distinctly heard chanting forth the glorious old hymn of victory, intoned loud and clear to tell the world how 'Christ is risen from the dead,' having trampled death beneath His feet, and henceforth they that are in the tombs have everlasting life."

"While Thee I Seek, Protecting Power"
Helen Maria Williams

HELEN MARIA WILLIAMS, who wrote this
hymn, was one of the most brilliant women
of the eighteenth and nineteenth centuries. She
was the daughter of an officer in the British army,
and was born in 1762, some say in London, but
probably at or near Berwick-on-Tweed, in the north
of England.

Obtaining a good education, Miss Williams began
to write poetry very early, and published her first
book at the age of twenty. It was followed by
many others, fiction, science, translation, poetry, and
especially books dealing with the French revolution.

Following her sister, who married a French Prot-
estant, Miss Williams spent most of her life in Paris.
She sympathized strongly with the republicans, and
was so outspoken that she was imprisoned by
Robespierre, and was not released until his death.
She herself died in 1827.

Miss Williams, in spite of her intense interest in
the politics of that tumultuous period, was a woman
of deep spiritual feeling, as we may well understand
from our hymn, which is the only piece, out of all
her many writings, to survive in common interest.
It was written in 1786, and was perhaps prophetic of
" the gathering storm" of the French revolution,

during which she must often have been helped by this very hymn to seek, in peril and prison, the Protecting Power.   The hymn is as follows :—

> While Thee I seek, protecting Power !
>   Be my vain wishes stilled ;
> And may this consecrated hour
>   With better hopes be filled.
> Thy love the power of thought bestowed ;
>   To Thee my thoughts would soar ;
> Thy mercy o'er my life has flowed ;
>   That mercy I adore.
>
> In each event of life how clear
>   Thy ruling hand I see !
> Each blessing to my soul more dear
>   Because conferred by Thee.
> In every joy that crowns my days,
>   In every pain I bear,
> My heart shall find delight in praise
>   Or seek relief in prayer.
>
> When gladness wings my favored hour,
>   Thy love my thoughts shall fill ;
> Resigned, when storms of sorrow lower,
>   My soul shall meet Thy will.
> My lifted eye, without a tear,
>   The gathering storm shall see ;
> My steadfast heart shall know no fear ;
>   That heart shall rest on Thee.

"I Love Thy Kingdom, Lord!"
Timothy Dwight

THE leader of early American hymn-writers was Rev. Timothy Dwight, D. D. He was born in Northampton, Mass., May 14, 1752, graduated from Yale in 1769 at the early age of seventeen, taught there as a tutor for six years, became an army chaplain during the Revolution, and then a Connecticut pastor and academy teacher, and finally, in 1795, was made president of Yale College, a post which he held with great honor. When he ceased to be a tutor there, the students had unanimously voted for him as president. He was a notable scholar, and did much for the reputation of the new republic in Europe. His literary work was done with an amanuensis, since his sight failed him on account of smallpox, with which, after the fashion of those days before vaccination, he was deliberately *inoculated*. He was always a great sufferer from pain in his eyes and the front of his brain, and seldom could read consecutively more than fifteen minutes a day—often not at all. He died January 11, 1817.

Dr. Dwight wrote 33 hymns, the one we are to commit to memory being by far the best and the most popular. It was published in 1800, as part of an edition of Watts's Psalms, which he edited at the request of the General Association of Connecticut. The thought of the hymn is that of Psalm 137. There were originally eight stanzas, but the following five are all that are now sung.

I love Thy kingdom, Lord !
  The house of Thine abode,
The church our blest Redeemer saved
  With His own precious blood.

I love Thy church, O God!
  Her walls before Thee stand,
Dear as the apple of Thine eye,
  And graven on Thy hand.

For her my tears shall fall,
  For her my prayers ascend ;
To her my cares and toils be given,
  Till toils and cares shall end.

Beyond my highest joy
  I prize her heavenly ways,
Her sweet communion, solemn vows,
  Her hymns of love and praise.

Sure as Thy truth shall last,
  To Zion shall be given
The brightest glories earth can yield,
  And brighter bliss of heaven.

"Hail! Columbia"

Joseph Hopkinson

EVERY American should commit to memory this patriotic song, which many consider to be our national anthem. It was written by Judge Joseph Hopkinson, a leading American of the early days of the United States. He was born in Philadelphia, November 12, 1770, and his boyhood was thrilled by the news 'of the Revolutionary War and the establishment of the new nation. His father, Francis Hopkinson, was also a famous lawyer, and was one of the signers of the Declaration of Independence. He wrote much, in prose and verse.

His distinguished son was graduated from the University of Pennsylvania, became a famous lawyer, a member of Congress, and a United States District judge, as his father and grandfather had been before him. He died in Philadelphia, January 15, 1842.

"Hail! Columbia" was written in 1798. At that time there was intense feeling throughout America with regard to the conduct of France toward this country, and there was prospect of war with the former friend of the United States. At that time Mr. Fox, a young singer in a Philadelphia theatre, was to have a benefit, and there was no indication of a full house. To arouse interest he got Judge

Hopkinson to write a patriotic song to the music of "The President's March." The song was "Hail! Columbia," which is still sung to the original tune. It was immediately successful. Mr. Fox was recalled nine times to sing the song, and at the last time the whole audience rose and sung the chorus. On the following night, April 30, President John Adams and his wife were present, and the singer was called back again and again. All the places of public assembly took up the song, and it was everywhere sung in the streets. One night a crowd gathered in front of Judge Hopkinson's house, and five hundred voices suddenly broke out with "Hail! Columbia."

The song is largely a glorification of George Washington, who, in that emergency, had been called from private life once more to take command of the American army. The last stanza refers to this.

Hail, Columbia! happy land!
Hail, ye heroes! heaven-born band!
 Who fought and bled in Freedom's cause,
 Who fought and bled in Freedom's cause,
And when the storm of war was gone,
Enjoyed the peace your valor won.
 Let independence be our boast,
 Ever mindful what it cost;
 Ever grateful for the prize,
 Let its altar reach the skies.

 Firm, united let us be,
 Rallying round our Liberty;
 As a band of brothers joined,
 Peace and safety we shall find.

Immortal patriots ! rise once more :
Defend your rights, defend your shore :
  Let no rude foe, with impious hand,
  Let no rude foe, with impious hand,
Invade the shrine where sacred lies
Of toil and blood the well-earned prize.
  While offering peace sincere and just
  In heaven we place a manly trust,
  That truth and justice will prevail,
  And every scheme of bondage fail.

        Firm, united, etc.

Sound, sound, the trump of Fame !
Let Washington's great name
  Ring through the world with loud applause,
  Ring through the world with loud applause;
Let every clime to Freedom dear
Listen with a joyful ear.
  With equal skill, and godlike power,
  He governed in the fearful hour
  Of horrid war ; or guides, with ease,
  The happier times of honest peace.

        Firm, united, etc.

Behold the chief who now commands,
  Once more to serve his country, stands —
  The rock on which the storm will beat,
  The rock on which the storm will beat;
But, armed in virtue firm and true,
His hopes are fixed on heaven and you.
  When hope was sinking in dismay,
  And glooms obscured Columbia's day,
  His steady mind, from changes free,
  Resolved on death or liberty.

Firm, united let us be,
Rallying round our Liberty;
As a band of brothers joined,
Peace and safety we shall find.

"The Sands of Time Are Sinking"

Annie Ross Cousin

THIS beautiful hymn was written by Mrs. Annie Ross Cousin, a Scotch lady, the wife of Rev. William Cousin, minister of the Free Church of Melrose, Scotland. The hymn was first published in 1857.

It is often called "Rutherford's Hymn," because it represents the thoughts and even quotes the very words of the great Scottish scholar, preacher, reformer, and martyr, Samuel Rutherford. Rutherford was born in 1600 and died in prison in 1661. He was a man of profound piety and great learning, highly honored among the Presbyterians. During Cromwell's time he was happy in the success of the principles for which he had pleaded courageously for many years ; but when Charles the Second came to the throne his enemies had their revenge. He was indicted for treason, and would have been executed if he had not died in prison.

Late in the afternoon of the last day of his life this sainted hero, in answer to the question, "What think ye now of Christ?" made the following answer, which furnished the refrain of our hymn : "Oh, that all my brethren in the land may know what a Master I have served, and what peace I have this

184

day ! I shall sleep in Christ, and when I awake, I shall be satisfied with His likeness. This night shall close the door, and put my anchor within the veil ; and I shall go away in a sleep by five of the clock in the morning. Glory ! glory to my Creator and my Redeemer forever ! I shall live and adore Him. Oh, for arms to embrace Him ! Oh, for a well-tuned harp ! Glory ! glory dwelleth in Immanuel's land !" He died exactly at the time he had fore-told.

Mrs. Cousin wrote many beautiful hymns and other poems, but this is by far the best known. It is really a poem, of 19 double stanzas, 152 lines, and only a small portion of it is ever sung. We give the part generally used as a hymn :—

The sands of time are sinking ;
　The dawn of heaven breaks ;
The summer morn I've sighed for,
　The fair, sweet morn, awakes.
Dark, dark hath been the midnight ;
　But dayspring is at hand,
And glory—glory dwelleth
　In Immanuel's land.

O Christ ! He is the fountain,
　The deep, sweet well of love ;
The streams on earth I've tasted,
　More deep I'll drink above ;
There to an ocean fulness
　His mercy doth expand,
And glory—glory dwelleth
　In Immanuel's land.

With mercy and with judgment
  My web of time He wove,
And aye the dews of sorrow
  Were lustred by His love ;
I'll bless the hand that guided,
  I'll bless the heart that planned,
When throned where glory dwelleth,
  In Immanuel's land.

The bride eyes not her garment,
  But her dear bridegroom's face ;
I will not gaze at glory,
  But on my King of Grace —
Not at the crown He giveth,
  But on His piercèd hand —
The Lamb is all the glory
  Of Immanuel's land.

"There Are Lonely Hearts to Cherish"
George Cooper

GEORGE COOPER, who wrote this helpful hymn, was born in New York City, May 14, 1840. He has written many poems and magazine articles, and not a few of his poems have become popular songs. He has written largely for children. This hymn, which is his best-known song, was written in 1870.

There are lonely hearts to cherish
　While the days are going by ;
There are weary souls who perish
　While the days are going by ;
If a smile we can renew,
As our journey we pursue,
O, the good we all may do
　While the days are going by.

There's no time for idle scorning
　While the days are going by ;
Let your face be like the morning
　While the days are going by ;
O, the world is full of sighs,
Full of sad and weeping eyes ;
Help your fallen brother rise
　While the days are going by.

All the loving links that bind us
   While the days are going by
One by one we leave behind us
   While the days are going by;
But the seeds of good we sow
Both in shade and shine will grow,
And will keep our hearts aglow
   While the days are going by.

"What Shall the Harvest Be?"
Emily Sullivan Oakey

THIS beautiful and beloved hymn was written in 1850 by Mrs. Emily Sullivan Oakey, who wrote much for the newspapers and magazines, but who is best known by this hymn. Mrs. Oakey was a teacher of languages and English literature, and taught all her life in the school from which she was graduated, the Albany (N. Y.) Female Academy. She was born in Albany on October 8, 1829, and died on May 11, 1883. She was frail in body, and it is said that during all her life she never enjoyed a day of good health.

This was the hymn that saved W. O. Lattimore, a man who had learned to drink in the army, and who found himself in the winter of 1876 a miserable drunkard, separated from his wife and child, stumbling by mistake, half intoxicated, into Moody's Tabernacle in Chicago. When he discovered his mistake he was about to go out, but Mr. Sankey's voice held him. He was singing this hymn:—

> Sowing the seed of a lingering pain,
> Sowing the seed of a maddened brain,
> Sowing the seed of a tarnished name,
> Sowing the seed of eternal shame:
>   O, what shall the harvest be?

Those words followed Lattimore even to the saloon, brought him back to the Tabernacle, and finally led to his conversion. He was reunited to his family, became an efficient laborer in the Moody meetings, was persuaded to study for the ministry, and served for twenty years as the honored and useful pastor of a large church in Evanston, Ill.

Mrs. Oakey's hymn may have been suggested by the parable of the sower or that of the tares, but more likely the writer had in mind Gal. 6 : 7 : "Whatsoever a man soweth, that shall he also reap."

Here is the hymn : —

Sowing the seed by the daylight fair,
Sowing the seed by the noonday glare,
Sowing the seed by the fading light,
Sowing the seed in the solemn night :
    O, what shall the harvest be ?

CHORUS :

Sown in the darkness or sown in the light,
Sown in our weakness or sown in our might,
Gathered in time or eternity,
Sure, ah, sure will the harvest be.

Sowing the seed by the wayside high,
Sowing the seed on the rocks to die,
Sowing the seed where the thorns will spoil,
Sowing the seed in the fertile soil :
    O, what shall the harvest be ?

Sowing the seed of a lingering pain,
Sowing the seed of a maddened brain,
Sowing the seed of a tarnished name,
Sowing the seed of eternal shame :
    O, what shall the harvest be ?

Sowing the seed with an aching heart,
Sowing the seed while the tear-drops start,
Sowing in hope till the reapers come
Gladly to gather the harvest home :
    O, what shall the harvest be ?

" The God of Abraham Praise "

Thomas Olivers

THE author of this Thanksgiving hymn was Rev. Thomas Olivers, who was born in Tregynon, Montgomeryshire, Wales, in 1725. His father and mother died when he was a young boy, and one person after another took charge of him, giving him little care. He grew up ignorant, irreligious, bad-tempered, and wicked. He became a shoemaker's apprentice. Making low acquaintances, he was driven from his native town at the age of 18, and wandered from place to place.

At last he came to Bristol, where the famous evangelist, George Whitefield, was preaching, and winning converts by the thousand. One day he preached from Zech. 3 : 2, " Is not this a brand plucked from the fire? " The godless cobbler heard him, and, as he said, " The world was all changed for Tom Olivers." From that time he devoted himself, in his own words, to " getting and doing good." He fasted long, and prayed by the hour, till his knees grew stiff and he was lame for some time.

Whitefield and his associates did not recognize the ability of Olivers, but on October 1, 1753, he met John Wesley, who made him a close associate in his ministry. In his preaching tours in England and Ireland he traveled 100,000 miles. He was worn by poverty, cares, and persecution, but was upheld by

a fervent faith.   He thought he had visions of Christ,
and rejoiced in them.   He died in London in March,
1799, and was buried in Wesley's tomb.

Olivers wrote other hymns, among them " Come,
immortal King of glory " and " O Thou God of my
salvation "; but the hymn we have chosen is the
most famous.   Originally it contained twelve eight-
line stanzas, but now only three of them are generally sung.

The inspiration for the hymn came from a Jew,
Meyer Lyon, chorister of the Great Synagogue in
London.   Olivers heard him sing the Hebrew creed
in thirteen articles, the Yigdal or Doxology, written
a thousand years ago, it is said, by Daniel ben Judah,
and still sung every Friday night in all synagogues
in the world.   For this tune, called " Leoni " out of
compliment to Meyer Lyon, Olivers wrote his splendid words.

The hymn has had a notable history.   Missionaries have admired it greatly, among them the famous Henry Martyn, who was much moved by it on
his voyage to India, and strove to make its sentiments his own.   The hymn was a favorite of the
poet Montgomery.   The great commentator, Dr.
Adam Clark, taught the hymn to all his children ;
one of them is known to have remembered it at the
age of eighty.

This hymn, which had, in a sense, a Hebrew origin,
is beautifully connected with a young Jewess, the
daughter of the chief of a synagogue, who became a
Christian and was baptized.   Her enraged father
vowed to kill her, and she took refuge in the home

of the clergyman who baptized her.   There, weeping, her eyes raised to heaven, she sung this hymn of praise to the God of Abraham, made manifest in Jesus Christ her Saviour.

The hymn, as it is now commonly sung, is as follows : —

> The God of Abraham praise,
>   Who reigns enthroned above,
> Ancient of everlasting days,
>   And God of love !
> Jehovah ! great I AM !
>   By earth and heaven confessed ;
> I bow and bless the sacred name,
>   Forever blest !
>
> The God of Abraham praise !
>   At whose supreme command
> From earth I rise, and seek the joys
>   At His right hand ;
> I all on earth forsake,
>   Its wisdom, fame, and power,
> And Him my only portion make,
>   My shield and tower.
>
> The God of Abraham praise !
>   Whose all-sufficient grace
> Shall guide me all my happy days
>   In all my ways :
> He calls a worm His friend !
>   He calls Himself my God !
> And He shall save me to the end
>   Through Jesus' blood !

"There's a Song in the Air"
Josiah Gilbert Holland

THIS beautiful Christmas hymn was written by the well-known poet and novelist, Josiah Gilbert Holland. He was born in Belchertown, Mass., July 24, 1819, and died in New York on October 12, 1881. Mr. Holland became first a physician, then a teacher, and finally found his life-work as an editor. Until 1866 he was a member of the editorial staff of that admirable newspaper, the Springfield (Mass.) *Republican*. In the columns of the *Republican* appeared Dr. Holland's "Timothy Titcomb Letters," whose quaint humor and sturdy common sense won for them universal favor. They appeared in book form in 1858, and several volumes of similar writing followed them.

Dr. Holland planned *Scribner's Magazine*, and edited that famous magazine from the beginning till his death. In it appeared some of his novels, the most popular of these being that strong and delightful story, "Arthur Bonnicastle," which still retains its popularity.

Dr. Holland wrote four or five volumes of poems, the most popular being "Bitter Sweet," a beautiful idyl of home life. Other long poems of similar theme are "Kathrina" and "The Mistress of the Manse."

195

Dr. Holland's Christmas poem, which immediately became a great Sunday-school favorite, is as follows: —

> There's a song in the air !
> There's a star in the sky !
> There's a mother's deep prayer
> And a baby's low cry !
> And the star rains its fire while the Beautiful sing,
> For the manger of Bethlehem cradles a king.

> There's a tumult of joy
> O'er the wonderful birth,
> For the virgin's sweet boy
> Is the Lord of the earth.
> Ay ! the star rains its fire and the Beautiful sing,
> For the manger of Bethlehem cradles a king.

> In the light of that star
> Lie the ages impearled ;
> And that song from afar
> Has swept over the world.
> Every hearth is aflame, and the Beautiful sing
> In the homes of the nations that Jesus is King.

> We rejoice in the light,
> And we echo the song
> That comes down through the night
> From the heavenly throng.
> Ay ! we shout to the lovely evangel they bring,
> And we greet in His cradle our Saviour and King.

"When Morning Gilds the Skies"
Edward Caswall

"WHEN morning gilds the skies" is by Edward Caswall, who was born in Yately, England, July 15, 1814. He was the son of a vicar of the Church of England, graduated at Oxford, and himself became a clergyman of the English Church. In 1847, however, he left that church and became a Catholic priest in the Birmingham church founded by Cardinal Newman, where he remained until his death, January 2, 1878.

He was very earnest in his duties as a minister, and took a loving interest in the poor, the sick, and little children. He translated many Latin hymns, and his work as a translator has obtained more favor than that of any one else except Dr. Neale. His translations are true to the original and are faultless in their form. The most famous of them are, " O Jesus, King most wonderful," and " Jesus, the very thought of Thee." Of the latter hymn Dr. Robinson says: " One might call this poem the finest in the world and still be within the limits of all extravagance."

Our hymn, " When morning gilds the skies," was written in 1854. It is a translation from a German hymn, but so free a translation that it is practically a new hymn. The hymn is said to be a great favorite in St. Paul's Cathedral, London, where it is usually

printed for distribution on a separate sheet.   The
following is the entire hymn : —

When morning gilds the skies,
My heart, awaking, cries,
    May Jesus Christ be praised !
Alike at work and prayer,
To Jesus I repair ;
    May Jesus Christ be praised !

Whene'er the sweet church-bell
Peals over hill and dell,
    May Jesus Christ be praised !
O, hark to what it sings
As joyously it rings,
    May Jesus Christ be praised !

My tongue shall never tire
Of chanting with the choir,
    May Jesus Christ be praised !
This song of sacred joy,
It never seems to cloy ;
    May Jesus Christ be praised !

When sleep her balm denies,
My silent spirit sighs,
    May Jesus Christ be praised !
When evil thoughts molest,
With this I shield my breast :
    May Jesus Christ be praised !

Does sadness fill my mind,
A solace here I find :
    May Jesus Christ be praised !
Or fades my earthly bliss,
My comfort still is this :
    May Jesus Christ be praised !

The night becomes as day,
When from the heart we say,
  May Jesus Christ be praised !
The powers of darkness fear
When this sweet chant they hear:
  May Jesus Christ be praised !

In heaven's eternal bliss
The loveliest strain is this:
  May Jesus Christ be praised !
Let earth, and sea, and sky
From depth to height reply,
  May Jesus Christ be praised !

Be this, while life is mine,
My canticle divine:
  May Jesus Christ be praised !
Be this the eternal song
Through ages all along:
  May Jesus Christ be praised !

"Somebody Did a Golden Deed"

John R. Clements

THIS famous song was written by that well-known
Christian Endeavorer, Mr. John R. Clements.
Born in County Armagh, Ireland, November 28,
1868, of Scotch-Irish parents, John Clements was
brought to the United States at the age of two. He
lived in the country till he was seventeen years old,
and got his education in "the old schoolhouse on
the hill."

He began business at the age of thirteen, and has
been at it ever since. For four years a retail grocery-
clerk, he has since been in the wholesale grocery
business, and is very successful.

Mr. Clements was "born again" under Mr.
Moody's preaching in 1886. He is a Presbyterian
deacon in his home city of Binghamton, N. Y.

As Mr. Clements says, he was "discovered, developed, and educated by, through, and in Christian
Endeavor." He became the president of the New
York State Christian Endeavor Union. He served
faithfully for many years as the secretary of that
union, and has back of him a long record of Christian Endeavor service in all kinds of positions—in
local societies, local unions, and the State union. He
has spoken at many International Conventions also,
and he is always ready to aid the Christian Endeavor
cause.

Mr. Clements is still a young man, in age and force, in spite of the large amount of work he has done. He is a very devoted Bible student, and practically all of his hymns took their suggestion from the Book of books. A man of the cheeriest and most friendly temper, he is an inspiring speaker, a warm personal friend, and an enthusiastic and resourceful religious leader.

Mr. Clements began to write verse at the age of fifteen,—" because I could not help it," he says ; and adds, " Christian Endeavor put the devotional touch to my pen." He has probably written more hymns than any other Christian Endeavorer, and he has edited several song-books, especially " Best Endeavor Hymns," which he edited with Mr. I. Allan Sankey, the son of the famous singer. Some of the best music for Mr. Clements's hymns was written by Professor Weeden, a life-long friend of Mr. Clements. Another of his close friends among song-writers is Fanny Crosby.

Among the well-known songs written by Mr. Clements are "Jesus Leads," " No Night There," " Until a Little While," " Lord, Is It I ? " and " Just a Little Sunshine," but the most famous of his songs is, " Somebody Did a Golden Deed."

The first stanza was not written by Mr. Clements, but is part of an anonymous poem which he found, using only the first stanza, and revising that. The remainder of the poem is entirely Mr. Clements's. Professor Weeden, who wrote the music, considered it to be his best song-tune.

Mr. Clements says that the song grew out of a

discouraging personal Christian experience. Mr. Alexander made much use of the song in his London evangelistic campaign with Dr. Torrey, and many testimonies have come to Mr. Clements regarding the power of the song in distant lands. The stanzas are as follows :—

> Somebody did a golden deed,
> Proving himself a friend in need ;
> Somebody sang a cheerful song,
> Brightening the skies the whole day long,—
>   Was that somebody you ?

> Somebody thought 'tis sweet to live,
> Willingly said, " I'm glad to give " ;
> Somebody fought a valiant fight,
> Bravely he lived to shield the right,—
>   Was that somebody you ?

> Somebody made a loving gift,
> Cheerfully tried a load to lift ;
> Somebody told the love of Christ,
> Told how His will was sacrificed,—
>   Was that somebody you ?

> Somebody idled all the hours,
> Carelessly crushed life's fairest flowers ;
> Somebody made life loss, not gain,
> Thoughtlessly seemed to live in vain,—
>   Was that somebody you ?

> Somebody filled the days with light,
> Constantly chased away the night ;
> Somebody's work bore joy and peace,
> Surely his life shall never cease,—
>   Was that somebody you ?

"O God, the Rock of Ages"

Edward Henry Bickersteth

THIS beautiful hymn was written by Edward Henry Bickersteth, who was born at Islington, England, on January 25, 1825. His father was a clergyman of the English Church, and was himself an able hymn-writer and editor of hymn-books. The son was educated at Cambridge University— which afterward gave him the degree of Doctor of Divinity—and rose in the English Church until he became in 1885 Bishop of Exeter. He held that position for fifteen years, greatly honored and beloved, and resigned in 1900. He died on May 16, 1906.

Bishop Bickersteth wrote twelve volumes, chiefly poems. One of these was a long poem, occupying twelve cantos, or books, in blank verse. It is entitled, "Yesterday, To-day, and Forever"—a lofty theme, dealing with the past, the present, and the future.

Bishop Bickersteth edited three hymnals, and thirty of his own hymns have come into common use. All of them are full of deep feeling and are particularly suited to the uses of private devotion. Among his best-loved hymns are "Peace, perfect peace," "'Till He come,' oh, let the words," "O Christ, who hast ascended," "Not worthy, Lord, to gather up the crumbs," and " Stand, soldier of the cross."

Our hymn, " O God, the Rock of Ages," was composed in 1862. The author associated it with Isa. 40 : 8 in printing it, stating that that verse suggested the hymn ; but the hymn is almost a literal and very beautiful rendering of the Ninetieth Psalm. It is as follows :—

O God, the Rock of Ages,
  Who evermore hast been,
What time the tempest rages,
  Our dwelling-place serene ;
Before Thy first creations,
  O Lord, the same as now,
To endless generations
  The Everlasting Thou.

Our years are like the shadows
  On sunny hills that lie,
Or grasses in the meadows
  That blossom but to die :
A sleep, a dream, a story
  By strangers quickly told,
An unremaining glory
  Of things that soon are old.

O Thou, who canst not slumber,
  Whose light grows never pale,
Teach us aright to number
  Our years before they fail.
On us Thy mercy lighten,
  On us Thy goodness rest,
And let Thy spirit brighten
  The hearts Thyself hast blessed.

Lord, crown our faith's endeavor
  With beauty and with grace,
Till, clothed in light forever,
  We see Thee face to face :
A joy no language measures,
  A fountain brimming o'er,
An endless flow of pleasures,
  An ocean without shore.

" Lord, It Belongs Not to My Care "
Richard Baxter

RICHARD BAXTER, who wrote this beautiful hymn, was a famous English clergyman and author. He was born on November 12, 1615, in one of the most troublous times of English history. He was converted at the age of fifteen by watching the beautiful way in which his father, when oppressed and persecuted, faced and conquered his enemies.

Baxter became a school-teacher, and then a minister of the Church of England. At one time he was the chaplain of one of Cromwell's regiments. After the monarchy was restored, he became chaplain to Charles the Second, and was so honored that a bishopric was offered to him, but he refused it.

There came a time, however, when restrictions were placed upon the clergymen of the English Church, and Baxter, with two thousand other " Nonconformists " who would not agree to these requirements, were in 1662 driven from their churches, and from that time for many years Baxter was subject to severe persecutions.

Once he was imprisoned for a year and a half. At another time a friend left him in his will $100 to distribute his book, " A Call to the Unconverted," but the courts held the legacy void, as it was to be applied "to superstitious uses." At one time a guard of soldiers prevented his entering his pulpit. At another time, because it would have been his death to put him in prison, he was heavily fined for the preaching of five sermons, and his goods and his books were sold to pay the fine. He was brought into court at another time for the writing of a paraphrase of the New Testament. His appearance was so sad, yet dignified, that the eyes of Judge Hale filled with tears when Baxter was brought before him.

Baxter died on December 8, 1691. He wrote sixty large volumes and more than one hundred pamphlets; he also wrote several volumes of poems. One of them, which contained the hymn we are studying, was published in 1681 with the curious title: "Poetical Fragments: Heart Imployment with God and Itself: The Concordant Discord of a Broken-healed Heart: Sorrowing-rejoicing, Fearing-hoping, Dying-living."

The hymn was originally one of eight stanzas, with eight lines each. Our five-stanza hymn, of four lines each, is taken from it.

The hymn was entitled by Baxter, "The Covenant and Confidence of Faith," and he affixed to the hymn the following tender note: "This Covenant my dear Wife in her former Sickness subscribed with a Cheerful will."

Baxter's greatest prose work was his "Saint's Everlasting Rest," usually referred to as "Baxter's Saint's Rest." The book was written at a time when Mr. Baxter himself was withdrawn from work because of physical weakness, and compelled to rest. Baxter's "Call," the fuller title being the "Call to the Unconverted," is another famous work from his pen.

Mr. Baxter was a most faithful pastor. When he went to his first charge it is said that hardly a house on a street was in the practice of family prayers. When he left, there was hardly a household that did not observe the custom.

In his last illness, when a caller asked how he was, he looked up to heaven and said, "Almost well."

Here is his most beautiful poem :—

> Lord, it belongs not to my care
>   Whether I die or live ;
> To love and serve Thee is my share,
>   And this Thy grace must give.

> If life be long, I will be glad
>   That I may long obey ;
> If short, yet why should I be sad
>   To soar to endless day ?

> Christ leads me through no darker rooms
>   Than He went through before ;
> No one into His kingdom comes
>   But through His open door.

> Come, Lord, when grace has made me meet
>   Thy blessed face to see ;
> For if Thy work on earth be sweet,
>   What will Thy glory be !

My knowledge of that life is small ;
  The eye of faith is dim ;
But 'tis enough that Christ knows all,
  And I shall be with Him.

"O Lord, How Full of Sweet Content"

Madame Guyon

ONE of the most remarkable women who ever lived was Madame Jeanne Marie Bouvières de la Mothe Guyon. She was born in Montargis, France, April 13, 1648, and was educated in a convent. At the early age of sixteen she married M. Guyon, a man twenty-two years older than herself.

Her married life was full of trials, on account of the poor health of her husband, the harshness of her mother-in-law combined with her own quick temper, the death of a child at the age of four, and the loss of her beauty through smallpox at the age of twenty-two.

After twelve years of this unhappy married life her husband died. Madame Guyon then appointed a guardian for her three children, settled the most of her property upon them, and as an ardent Catholic spent the rest of her life in religious meditation and active teaching.

She was an earnest devotee of what is known as Quietism, a form of religion consisting of contemplation of God and the reception of His Spirit, the attempt being made to withdraw the soul from everything else so that it is oblivious alike of good and of evil, and does not even care whether it is saved or lost.

Such a system of thought leads its followers to be entirely careless of all outward acts, and Madame Guyon was often assailed by scandals, which were probably unfounded.   Her teaching was opposed by the church, and she was compelled to promise to cease advocating her peculiar views, but she broke the promise.   She was imprisoned three times, the last time in the famous Bastile in Paris for four years. She was kept in one of the darkest dungeons, in the same tower where the famous unknown prisoner, "the Man with the Iron Mask," was confined—a prisoner whose face was always hidden by a mask.

Madame Guyon wrote forty volumes.   Among these were no fewer than nine hundred hymns and other poems, many of which were written in prison. She would sometimes write five or six hymns in a single day.   She was a woman of most attractive personality, and her life was filled with deeds of charity.   After all her troubles she died in peace at Diziers on June 9, 1717.

Our hymn is said to have been written in 1681, when Madame Guyon was thirty-three years old. She was then living near Geneva, at a distance from her home, and the last stanza refers to that fact.

The hymn was translated from the French by William Cowper.   A friend gave him Madame Guyon's poems to translate at a time when he himself was in one of his fits of deep melancholy approaching insanity, hoping that the calm taught by Madame Guyon would enter his own life.   In all,

Cowper translated thirty-seven of her hymns, this being by far the most famous. The original poem had nine stanzas, but only the following four are commonly used in our hymnals :—

O Lord, how full of sweet content
Our years of pilgrimage are spent !
Where'er we dwell, we dwell with **Thee,**
In heaven, in earth, or on the sea.

To us remains nor place nor time :
Our country is in every clime :
We can be calm and free from care
On any shore, since God is there.

While place we seek, or place we shun,
The soul finds happiness in none ;
But with our God to guide our way,
'Tis equal joy to go or stay.

Could we be cast where Thou art not,
That were indeed a dreadful lot ;
But regions none remote we call,
Secure of finding God in all.

"Cast Thy Burden on the Lord"
Rowland Hill

IT is not positively known that this hymn was written by Rowland Hill, but it is practically certain that Mr. Hill wrote the hymn in its first form and published it in 1783 in his collection, "Psalms and Hymns," with the title, "Encouragement for the Weak." The hymn was re-written by George Rawson in 1853, and we still use many of Rawson's changes.

When singing the hymn it is pleasant to connect it with Rowland Hill, who was one of the most interesting characters of modern times. He was born near Shrewsbury, England, August 23, 1744. His father was Sir Rowland Hill, who deserves the especial gratitude of the world for the improvements he made in regard to letter postage. Before his time postage had been very high. It varied according to the distance the letter had to be carried, and was paid, not by the sender of the letter, but by the recipient. Sir Rowland Hill changed all that. He invented perforated stamps, and brought about prepayment of postage, and a uniform and low rate.

His son Rowland, educated at Cambridge University, became a minister of the Church of England. Even while preparing for the ministry he scandalized his teachers by conducting religious services in the

homes of the poor and the sick.   He came under the
influence of George Whitefield, the famous evangelist, and himself took up the practice, so strange at
that time, of outdoor preaching.

He spent twelve years as an itinerant minister, and
then, falling heir to considerable property, he built
Surrey Chapel in London at his own expense, and
preached there for fifty years, until his death.   He
was very popular, and his congregations were the
largest in London.   It was his practice every summer to make extensive gospel tours.   He had a
strong voice, which fitted him for outdoor preaching,
and he was possessed of great dramatic power.   For
example, at one time he was impressed by the earnestness of a man who was selling matches outside
his study window, and began his next sermon by
shouting, " Matches !   Matches !   Matches !" at the
top of his voice, going on to preach concerning the
value of earnestness.   He was a man of tremendous
energy, and preached on the average 350 sermons
a year for sixty-six years.   He was in the habit of
declaring that any man who had become able to
preach extemporaneously should find preaching a
daily delight.

Mr. Hill was greatly interested in missions and
evangelism.   He was one of the founders of the London Missionary Society, and was a member of the
first committee of the Religious Tract Society.

He was a famous wit and was remarkable for his
eccentricity.   At one time after a group in which he
was present had been indulging in considerable
scandal he called for a brush and dust-pan and be-

gan to sweep the floor, declaring that a good deal of dirt had been scattered around there lately.

On another occasion when a frank critic after listening to Mr. Hill declared that the sermon had gone "from Dan to Beer-sheba," "Never mind, my friend," the preacher answered, "that is all holy ground."

"I like ejaculatory prayer," he once said, "it reaches heaven before the devil can get a shot at it."

He cared more for the matter than for the manner of his speech. "Those who are hearing a will read," he argued, "consider the contents rather than the manner in which it is read."

He was strongly evangelistic. "A sermon is not worth a rush," he declared, "that has not got the Redeemer in it."

He was possessed of a beautiful Christian spirit, well expressed in one of his well-known sayings, "The best of life is to live for others." "Every twig of God's rod," he said, "grows in the paradise of His love."

Mr. Hill came to the close of his useful life on April 11, 1833. He wrote several hymn-books, and a number of works in prose. To the hymn-books he contributed a number of hymns, but all of them anonymously. Our hymn is the most famous of these. Its thought, of course, is derived from Psalm 55 : 22, and the hymn is as follows :—

> Cast thy burden on the Lord,
> Only lean upon His word ;
> Thou shalt soon have cause to bless
> His eternal faithfulness.

Ever in the raging storm
Thou shalt see His cheering form,
Hear His pledge of coming aid :
" It is I, be not afraid."

Cast thy burden at His feet ;
Linger at His mercy-seat :
He will lead thee by the hand
Gently to the better land.

He will gird thee by His power,
In thy weary, fainting hour :
Lean, then, loving, on His word ;
Cast thy burden on the Lord.

" The Breaking Waves Dashed High "
Felicia Dorothea Hemans

MRS. HEMANS, who wrote this patriotic hymn, was one of the greatest women of the past century. She was Felicia Dorothea Browne, and was born in Liverpool, on September 25, 1793. She married Captain Hemans of the British army, but they lived together only six years. He ran away to Italy, leaving her with their five sons, and she never saw him again. This event greatly saddened her life, and, together with the hard work and anxiety attending the education of her children, hastened the disease of which she died on May 16, 1835, at the early age of forty-one.

Mrs. Hemans began to write creditable verse at the age of eleven, and published her first volume of poems when she was fifteen. Another book of hers, published the same year, won the praise of Shelley. Wordsworth called her

> " That holy spirit,
> Sweet as the spring, as ocean deep."

Once she visited Sir Walter Scott, and in parting the great writer said to her, " There are some whom we meet and should like ever after to claim as kith and kin, and you are one of these."

Mrs. Hemans wrote many books, and her poems had a very wide popularity. "The Forest Sanctuary" is probably the best of them. Especially famous are "Casabianca" ("The boy stood on the burning deck"), "The Voice of Spring," and "The Stately Homes of England."

Of her poems used as hymns the best known are, "Calm on the bosom of thy God," "Child amidst the flowers at play," "I hear thee speak of the better land," and the one we print below, "The breaking waves dashed high."

This brilliant poem, whose title is "The Landing of the Pilgrim Fathers in New England," was published in 1828. As she sat at the tea-table one evening Mrs. Hemans read an old account of the landing of the Pilgrims, and was at once moved to write the poem. James T. Fields, the poet and publisher, once visited her and obtained an autograph copy of the poem, which is now preserved in Pilgrim Hall in Plymouth, Mass.

The hymn is a long one, but it would be difficult to omit a stanza :—

> The breaking waves dashed high
>   On a stern and rock-bound coast,
> And the woods against a stormy sky
>   Their giant branches tossed ;
>
> And the heavy night hung dark
>   The hills and waters o'er,
> When a band of exiles moored their bark
>   On the wild New England shore.
>
> Not as the conqueror comes,
>   They, the true-hearted, came ;
> Not with the roll of the stirring drums,
>   And the trumpet that sings of fame ;

Not as the flying come,
  In silence and in fear ;
They shook the depths of the desert gloom
  With their hymns of lofty cheer.

Amidst the storm they sang,
  And the stars heard and the sea ;
And the sounding aisles of the dim woods rang
  To the anthem of the free !

The ocean eagle soared
  From his nest by the white wave's foam ;
And the rocking pines of the forest roared —
  This was their welcome home !

There were men with hoary hair
  Amidst that pilgrim band ;
Why had *they* come to wither there,
  Away from their childhood's land ?

There was woman's fearless eye,
  Lit by her deep love's truth ;
There was manhood's brow serenely high,
  And the fiery heart of youth.

What sought they thus afar ?—
  Bright jewels of the mine ?
The wealth of seas, the spoils of war ?—
  They sought a faith's pure shrine !

Ay, call it holy ground,
  The soil where first they trod,
They have left unstained what there they found —
  Freedom to worship God !

" There Is a Happy Land "

Andrew Young

ANDREW YOUNG, who wrote this favorite Sunday-school song, "There is a happy land," was the son of David Young, who was a very successful teacher in Edinburgh, Scotland, for more than fifty years.

Andrew was born in Edinburgh on April 23, 1907, and distinguished himself for his scholarship during his course in Edinburgh University. In 1830 he became head master of Niddry Street School in Edinburgh, where he began with eighty pupils, and in ten years increased the number to 600 pupils. In 1840 he became head master of Madras College in St. Andrew's University, where he met with equal success. In 1853 he retired and lived in Edinburgh until his death, November 30, 1889.

Mr. Young contributed to periodicals many hymns and other poems of admirable quality, and in 1876 he made a collection of those, entitled "Scottish Islands and Other Poems." The most popular of his hymns, "There is a happy land," was written in 1838, after Mr. Young had been spending the evening in the home of Mrs. Marshall, the mother of one of his pupils, who had played a Hindu air which he liked. The name was " Happy Land," and the tune so fastened itself in his head that he wrote his hymn to it. It was sung in his class at the Niddry Street School, and there it was heard by Rev. James Gall, who in 1843 included it in his " Sacred Song Book," where it soon became well known.

It was translated into Chinese, the languages of India, Africa, and many other lands. The famous Presbyterian missionary to the New Hebrides, Dr. John Inglis, translated it in 1854 into the language of those islands, and it became a great favorite there.

It is interesting to know that Mr. Young, whose hymn has been sung in almost every Sunday school in the world, was himself for some time the superintendent of a Sunday school in Edinburgh.

This is the hymn substantially as he wrote it :—

There is a happy land,
    Far, far away,
Where saints in glory stand,
    Bright, bright as day.
O, how they sweetly sing,
" Worthy is our Saviour King,
Loud let His praises ring,
    Praise, praise for aye."

Come to that happy land,
    Come, come away.
Why will ye doubting stand,
    Why still delay ?
O, we shall happy be
When, from sin and sorrow free,
Lord, we shall live with Thee,
    Blest, blest for aye.

Bright in that happy land
  Beams every eye.
Kept by a Father's hand,
  Love cannot die.
O, then to glory run ;
Be a crown and kingdom won ;
And bright, above the sun,
  We reign for aye.

"I Am So Glad That Our Father in Heaven"
P. P. Bliss

ONE of the leading hymn-writers of the United States was P. P. Bliss. Indeed, Mr. Bliss probably wrote more hymns that are held in high esteem by the church to-day than any other American, with the single exception of Fanny Crosby.

His life was one of exceptional interest. He was born in Clearfield County, Penn., July 9, 1838. His family was a poor one, living in a log house. His father removed several times to Ohio and back again to Pennsylvania, so that the lad had little schooling.

Mr. Bliss's name was originally "Philipp." Not relishing this eccentric spelling, Mr. Bliss in later years used the superfluous " P " as a middle initial, writing his name "Philip P. Bliss," or, more commonly, "P. P. Bliss."

His father taught him religion by his singing, praying, and Bible-reading, and every day his mother gave him lessons. Early in his boyhood he showed a passion for music, and would sing and play on rude instruments that he himself made. He was ten years old when he heard his first piano as he was passing by a house. The poor, barefoot boy was so fascinated that he dared to enter the house and stand at the parlor door. The young lady who was playing the piano stopped when she saw him. "O lady, play some more," said the boy ; but, far from being moved by his evident appreciation of the music, the young woman answered him rudely, "Get out of here with your great feet."

At the age of eleven young Bliss set out from his father's house to work on a farm, all his clothes being tied up in a handkerchief. At the age of thirteen we find him still working on a farm, getting the munificent wages of $9 a month. At the age of fourteen he was assistant cook in a lumber-camp, and the next year he began to cut logs, and then worked in a sawmill. During all this time he went to school when he could. In 1850 there was a revival in the schoolhouse, and, though he had always loved the Saviour, he then made public profession of his faith, and became a member of the Baptist church. In 1855 he had the rare privilege of a whole winter in school, and made so good use of his opportunity that the next year he himself taught a school. About this time he enjoyed his first singing-school, J. G. Towner being the teacher, and soon afterward he attended his first musical convention, in charge of the famous composer, W. B. Bradbury. Next we find him teaching in the academy of Rome, Penn.

He married, and his wife was indeed a helpmeet. She was a Presbyterian, and Mr. Bliss also joined that church, becoming the superintendent of the Sunday school. He heard of the Normal Academy of Music at Geneseo, N. Y., and longed to go so much that he broke down crying. He had not a cent in the world, and his wages were only $13 a month. Seeing his grief, his wife's grandmother brought out her stocking with its hoard of silver, a sum of more than $30, and gave it to him for that purpose. He became a music-teacher, and gave himself up to the fascinating art.

In 1864 he wrote and published his first song, "Lora Vale," and for the rest of his remaining twelve years of life he was writing songs and giving concerts, which were very popular. Mrs. Bliss went with him on his concert tours. He wrote many songs for Sunday-school books.

Meeting Mr. Moody, Major Whittle, and other evangelists, he himself became an evangelist, and was remarkably successful, especially with young people. He was on one of these evangelistic tours with his wife when both of them were killed in the great railroad disaster at Ashtabula, O., December 29, 1876. The train was precipitated by the fall of a bridge down a ravine sixty feet deep. The cars caught fire, and 100 of the passengers were killed. The death of Mr. and Mrs. Bliss under circumstances so tragic was a deep sorrow to the Christian world. He and his wife were greatly beloved wherever they were known, and his songs were sung everywhere, and have continued to be sung. Among the most famous of these are " Hold the fort," " Are your windows open toward Jerusalem?" " There's a light in the valley," " Only remembered by what I have done," " What shall the harvest be?" " Let the lower lights be burning," " Whosoever will," " Free from the law, oh, happy condition!" " Only an armor-bearer," " Pull for the shore," " Down life's dark vale we wander," " The light of the world is

Jesus," " Almost persuaded," "Hallelujah, 'tis done,"
" The half was never told," " More holiness give
me," " More to follow," " Daniel's Band," and " I
will sing of my Redeemer." To this last must be
added the hymn we have specially chosen, " I am so
glad that our Father in heaven." Of this hymn
Major Whittle, in his life of Mr. Bliss, writes as
follows :—

" I think it was in June, 1870, that ' Jesus loves
me ' was written. Mr. and Mrs. Bliss were at the
time members of my family, at 43 South May
Street, Chicago. One morning Mrs. Bliss came
down to breakfast, and said, as she entered the
room : ' Last evening Mr. Bliss had a tune given
him that I think is going to live and be one of the
most used that he has written. I have been singing
it all the morning to myself, and cannot get it out
of my mind.' She then sang over to us the notes
of 'Jesus loves me.' The idea of Mr. Bliss in writing
it was that the peace and comfort of a Christian
were not founded upon his loving Christ, but upon
Christ's love to him, and that to occupy the mind
with Christ's love would produce love and consecration in keeping with Rom. 5 : 5 : ' The love of God
[to us] is shed abroad in our hearts by the Holy
Ghost, which is given to us.' This view of gospel
truth was at this time being very preciously brought
to the souls of believers in Chicago by the preaching
of Moorhouse and Mr. Moody and by the Dublin
tracts and English commentaries upon gospel truth,
which, through Mr. Moody, began to be circulated
among Christians. How much God has used this

little song to lead sinners and fearful, timid Christians to 'look away to Jesus' eternity alone can tell."

Mr. Sankey had a beautiful experience with this song. A little girl, a member of his singing-class, lay dying, and as he was talking with her one day she said, "Don't you remember when you were teaching us to sing, 'I am so glad that Jesus loves me,' you told us that if we only gave our hearts to Him He would love us? and I did give my heart to Him." Mr. Sankey added, "What that little dying girl said to me helped to cheer me on more than anything I had heard before, because she was my first convert."

A missionary of the American Sunday School Union once sang that song in a meeting he was conducting in a small town in Missouri, where he had just organized a Sunday school. At the close of the song the missionary asked: "Are *you* glad? If not, why not?" On this a young man rushed up to the missionary, threw his arms about him, and said: "O, that song! I could not keep away from it, and it has saved me."

The hymn itself is as follows:—

> I am so glad that our Father in heaven
> Tells of His love in the Book He has given;
> Wonderful things in the Bible I see;
> This is the dearest, that Jesus loves me.

> *Chorus.*
> I am so glad that Jesus loves me,
> Jesus loves me, Jesus loves me;
> I am so glad that Jesus loves me,
> Jesus loves even me.

Though I forget Him and wander away,
Kindly He follows wherever I stray ;
Back to His dear loving arms would I flee,
When I remember that Jesus loves me.

O, if there's only one song I can sing,
When in His beauty I see the great King,
This shall my song in eternity be,
" O, what a wonder that Jesus loves me ! "

"When He Cometh"
William Orcutt Cushing

WILLIAM ORCUTT CUSHING, who signed his name to his hymns simply " W. O. Cushing," wrote a large number of songs that found wide popularity in Sunday school. He was born in Hingham, Mass., December 31, 1823, and died October 19, 1902.

Most of his songs are of death and heaven. The most familiar are, "Down in the valley with my Saviour I would go," " O, safe to the rock that is higher than I," "Ring the bells of heaven, there is joy to-day," "We are watching; we are waiting," and the "jewel song," "When He cometh," which is the one specially before us.

He wrote the "jewel song" when he was a young man, in 1856, and it was composed for use in his own Sunday school. George F. Root, the famous composer, wrote for it a very effective tune.

A minister once returning from Europe on a British steamer visited the steerage and proposed a song service there. He started it with this "jewel song." Mr. Root's melody was at once caught up by the immigrants, and they soon learned the hymn, which was sung by these men and women of all nations during the rest of the voyage. When at Quebec they took the train for their journeys to their new homes the song burst from every car.   Here are the words : —

When He cometh, when He cometh
To make up His jewels,
All the jewels, precious jewels,
His loved and His own ;
Like the stars of the morning,
His bright crown adorning,
They shall shine in their beauty,
Bright gems for His crown.

He will gather, He will gather
The gems for His kingdom,
All the pure ones, all the bright ones,
His loved and His own.

Like the stars, etc.

Little children, little children
Who love their Redeemer,
Are the jewels, precious jewels,
His loved and His own.

Like the stars, etc.

"Day by Day the Manna Fell"
Josiah Conder

JOSIAH CONDER, who wrote this beautiful hymn, was born in London, September 17, 1789. His father was a bookseller and engraver. When the boy was five years old he was inoculated for smallpox, and in the imperfect state of the practice he lost his right eye. His physician became interested in him, and taught the boy. At the age of fifteen he had progressed so far that he was able to enter his father's store as his assistant.

Conversation with the intelligent buyers that frequented the store led to young Conder's interest in literature. He became a well-known author, editor, and publisher, editing and owning *The Eclectic Review*, and editing a newspaper, *The Patriot*. He wrote many volumes of prose, travel, biography, and books on the Bible, and also six volumes of poems. His first volume of poems, " The Associate Minstrels," was written in conjunction with Ann and Jane Taylor and Eliza Thomas. The latter became his wife. The book was successful to the extent of going into a second edition.

Mr. Conder was one of the best of English hymn-writers. He was a Congregationalist, and, with the exception of Watts and Doddridge, wrote more hymns that are in common use than any other Congregational hymn-writer, about sixty of his hymns being still sung. The thought of his hymns is elevated, their language is beautiful, their style varied, their themes substantial, and their theology broad.

All his life he was compelled to struggle against pecuniary difficulties, but maintained his hope and trust. His hymns echo these trials, and echo also the Christian confidence with which he surmounted them.

He was a wise and successful editor of hymn-books, making many changes in the hymns that preceded him, and always to their advantage. Of his "Congregational Hymn-Book" 90,000 copies were sold in the first seven years, a remarkable sale for those days.

Mr. Conder died in London on December 27, 1855.

"Day by day the manna fell" appeared in 1836. It was based upon the line of the Lord's Prayer, "Give us day by day our daily bread." The entire hymn is as follows : —

> Day by day the manna fell:
> Oh, to learn this lesson well!
> Still by constant mercy fed,
> Give me, Lord, my daily bread.
> Day by day " the promise reads,
> Daily strength for daily needs;
> Cast foreboding fears away,
> Take the manna of to-day.
>
> Lord, my times are in Thy hand;
> All my sanguine hopes have planned
> To Thy wisdom I resign
> And would make Thy purpose mine.

Thou my daily task shalt give ;
Day by day to Thee I live :
So shall added years fulfil
Not mine own—my Father's will.

Fond ambition, whisper not ;
Happy is my humble lot.
Anxious, busy cares, away :
I'm provided for to-day.
Oh, to live exempt from care
By the energy of prayer :
Strong in faith, with mind subdued,
Yet elate with gratitude !

"Shout the Glad Tidings"

William Augustus Muhlenberg

THIS stirring and strikingly beautiful hymn was written by William Augustus Muhlenberg, D. D. Dr. Muhlenberg was the son of a clergyman and the grandson of the Muhlenberg who was the patriarch of the Lutheran church in America. He was born in Philadelphia, September 16, 1796, and was graduated in 1814 from the University of Pennsylvania. He became an Episcopal clergyman. At one time he was principal of St. John's College, Long Island. His greatest work was the founding, after long toil and courageous effort, of St. Luke's Hospital in New York City, which was established in 1859. He was its first pastor and superintendent, and continued in those offices until his death, which occurred on April 6, 1877.

Dr. Muhlenberg published a volume of poems in 1859. He wrote a number of exceedingly choice hymns, the most famous being, "I would not live alway," "Saviour! who Thy flock art feeding," and "Shout the glad tidings." The last-named hymn was written for Bishop Hobart, who wanted some verses that could be sung to the tune of "Avison," which was very popular as the tune of Moore's "Sound the loud timbrel." The entire hymn is as follows : —

Shout the glad tidings, exultingly sing ;
Jerusalem triumphs, Messiah is King.
Zion, the marvelous story be telling,
    The Son of the Highest, how lowly His birth ;
The brightest archangel in glory excelling,
    He stoops to redeem thee, He reigns upon earth.

Shout the glad tidings, exultingly sing ;
Jerusalem triumphs, Messiah is King.
Tell how He cometh ; from nation to nation,
    The heart-cheering news let the earth echo round ;
How free to the faithful He offers salvation !
    How His people with joy everlasting are crowned !

Shout the glad tidings, exultingly sing ;
Jerusalem triumphs, Messiah is King.
Mortals, your homage be gratefully bringing,
    And sweet let the gladsome hosanna arise ;
Ye angels, the full hallelujah be singing ;
    One chorus resound through the earth and the skies.

" Jesus, Saviour, Pilot Me "
Edward Hopper

THE author of this very popular hymn was Rev. Edward Hopper, D. D., who was born in New York City in 1818. His father was a merchant, and his mother was descended from the heroic Huguenots. He graduated from the University of the City of New York, and followed this with a course in Union Theological Seminary, from which he graduated in 1842.

For eleven years he was pastor of a Presbyterian church in Sag Harbor, Long Island, and then became pastor of a sailors' church in New York harbor, the Church of Sea and Land.

Lafayette College gave him the degree of doctor of divinity in 1871. It was in the same year that this hymn, "Jesus, Saviour, pilot me," was published in *The Sailors' Magazine*, and it was immediately printed in a hymn-book, "The Baptist Praise Book," published also in 1871.

Other hymns by Dr. Hopper are, "They pray the best who pray and watch," and "Wrecked and struggling in mid-ocean."

The original poem, "Jesus, Saviour, pilot me," contained six stanzas, but Dr. Hopper himself selected for use as a hymn the first and the last two stanzas, which are all that are ever sung. They are as follows : —

Jesus, Saviour, pilot me
Over life's tempestuous sea;
Unknown waves before me roll,
Hiding rock and treacherous shoal;
Chart and compass come from Thee:
Jesus, Saviour, pilot me.

As a mother stills her child,
Thou canst hush the ocean wild;
Boisterous waves obey Thy will
When Thou say'st to them, "Be still!"
Wondrous Sovereign of the sea,
Jesus, Saviour, pilot me.

When at last I near the shore,
And the fearful breakers roar
'Twixt me and the peaceful rest,
Then, while leaning on Thy breast,
May I hear Thee say to me,
"Fear not, I will pilot thee!"

" Let Us with a Gladsome Mind "

John Milton

THE author of this hymn is more famous than any other writer whose work we study in this book, for it is John Milton, the immortal author of "Paradise Lost." He was born in London, December 9, 1608, and died in the same city, November 8, 1674. He traveled widely in Europe, wrote some of his most beautiful poems when still a young man, and rose to great influence in the nation, becoming, under Cromwell and his successor, Latin secretary of state. He was engaged in these duties when he became blind, and it was in the retirement made necessary by this affliction that he composed "Paradise Lost" and "Paradise Regained."

Milton made metrical versions of nineteen Psalms, only two or three of which are sung in our day. Of these the most beautiful, as I think, is the thanksgiving hymn which is still one of the chief gems of our hymnals.

It is a version of Psalm 136, and was written in 1623, when Milton was only fifteen years old. The original translates the Psalm very fully, with almost as many stanzas as the Psalm has verses. The editors of our hymn-books have been obliged to make a selection, of course, and they have chosen wisely, though it is a pity to leave out of the hymn expressions of so great beauty as

" And caused the golden-tressèd sun
All day long his course to run."

" The hornèd moon to shine by night
Amongst her spangled sisters bright."

" He, with His thunder-clasping hand,
Smote the first-born of Egypt land."

The hymn-book editors have been obliged to make some changes in what they give, to adapt the verses to singing. I follow these, in the main, but keep more closely to the original than any hymn-book of my acquaintance.

Let us with a gladsome mind,
Praise the Lord, for He is kind ;
For His mercies aye endure,
Ever faithful, ever sure.

Let us blaze His name abroad,
For of gods He is the God ;
For His mercies aye endure,
Ever faithful, ever sure.

He, with all-commanding might,
Filled the new-made world with light ;
For His mercies aye endure,
Ever faithful, ever sure.

He His chosen race did bless
In the wasteful wilderness ;
For His mercies aye endure,
Ever faithful, ever sure.

He hath with a piteous eye,
Looked upon our misery ;
For His mercies aye endure,
Ever faithful, ever sure.

All things living He doth feed,
His full hand supplies their need ;
For His mercies aye endure,
Ever faithful, ever sure.

Let us therefore warble forth
His high majesty and worth ;
For His mercies aye endure,
Ever faithful, ever sure.

"We Give Thee Thanks, O God, This Day"

Robert M. Offord

THE author of this beautiful Thanksgiving hymn is Rev. Robert M. Offord, LL. D. He was born at St. Anstell, Cornwall, England, September 17, 1846. His father was a Baptist minister, who removed to London, dying there in 1869. The father was an intimate friend of Rev. C. H. Spurgeon, and the two occasionally filled each other's pulpits.

Coming on a visit to the United States, young Offord earned his living by literary work, and occasionally preached, as he had been doing in England under the auspices of the London Evangelistic Society. Later he was regularly ordained and became pastor of a church in Lodi, N. J., belonging to the Reformed Church in America. At the same time he became an editor of *The New York Observer*, where he served for eighteen years.

Dr. Offord is living now in Passaic, N. J., caring for various commercial interests, which give him little leisure for preaching.

Among the prime interests of Dr. Offord has been the Fulton Street noon prayer meeting, which he has attended between 3,000 and 4,000 times, for several years making a daily report for one journal and a weekly report for two or three others.

Among Dr. Offord's books is a unique collection of comments on Bible texts by 366 different ministers, one for every day of the year. This is entitled "Life's Golden Lamp." Dr. Offord also edited the life of Jerry McAuley, and twenty volumes of Dr. Talmage's sermons.

Amid his varied labors Dr. Offord has frequently found rest and comfort in writing hymns, most of which were published in *The New York Observer*. More than eighty of these he gathered into a little book entitled "Heart Song," copyrighted in 1895. In his introduction Dr. Theodore L. Cuyler said, "Mr. Offord writes in the same vein with the brothers Bonar."

The hymn by which Dr. Offord is best known was first published in *The New York Observer*, and then in the "Heart Song" collection.

"I have a great fondness for hymns," Dr. Offord writes me. "Who will say that we shall not sing new versions of 'Rock of Ages' and many other grand old earth melodies up in heaven?"

Here is Dr. Offord's Thanksgiving hymn:—

> We give Thee thanks, O God, this day,
>   For mercies never failing :
> Thy love hath brought us on our way
>   For all our wants availing.
>
> No less that love hath met our need
>   Than when the manna falling
> Did day by day Thy people feed,
>   To love and praises calling.

The smitten rock poured forth of old
　Its crystal waters gleaming ;
And still the same glad tale is told,
　For us the floods are streaming.

The seasons come, the seasons go,
　But each shall find us singing ;
For each shall greet us, well we know,
　New favors from Thee bringing.

Through endless years Thou art the same,
　Thy mercy changes never ;
Then blessed be Thy mighty name
　Forever and forever.

"Break Thou the Bread of Life"

Mary Artemisia Lathbury

MISS MARY ARTEMISIA LATHBURY, the author of this beautiful hymn, was born in Manchester, N. Y., August 10, 1841, the daughter of a Methodist minister. After leaving school she taught art for a while, and then became an editor, but after 1874 she devoted herself to general literary work and to drawing those exquisite pictures for which she was famous. She died in 1913.

She delighted especially to draw children, and the best periodicals for young folks, including *St. Nicholas*, were glad to print the products of her pencil. They were always delicately lovely, and whenever you saw " M. A. L." in a corner of a drawing you might be sure that it was one you would remember and want to return to again and again. Very serious difficulty with her eyes made her success as an artist doubly notable.

Miss Lathbury wrote books of her own, and illustrated many books by other writers.

She was a woman of great beauty of character, and every one loved her that came to know her. Her expressive face and gentle, modest bearing had a peculiar charm. She was intensely religious, and her personal devoutness is shown in her poems. She spent herself freely for others, and many owe much to her loving ministries.

Two of her hymns are known and loved everywhere. Both of these were written for Chautauqua, where they have become a part of the life of the institution, so that Miss Lathbury was known as the "lyrist of Chautauqua." One of these is the sweet evening hymn, "Day is dying in the west," written at the request of Bishop Vincent in the summer of 1880. The other—our present hymn—was written in the same year, for the Chautauqua Literary and Scientific Circle, and Miss Lathbury called it "A Study Song." Its lovely reference to the Sea of Galilee is made doubly interesting when one remembers that the hymn was written beside the beautiful Lake Chautauqua.

The hymn, which is very short, is as follows :—

> Break Thou the bread of life,
>   Dear Lord, to me,
> As Thou didst break the loaves
>   Beside the sea ;
> Beyond the sacred page
>   I seek Thee, Lord ;
> My spirit pants for Thee,
>   O Living Word !
>
> Bless Thou the truth, dear Lord,
>   To me—to me—
> As Thou didst bless the bread
>   By Galilee ;
> Then shall all bondage cease,
>   All fetters fall ;
> And I shall find my peace,
>   My All-in-All !

" Still, Still with Thee "
Harriet Beecher Stowe

MRS. HARRIET BEECHER STOWE was, with the exception of Queen Victoria, the most famous woman of the last half of the nineteenth century. She was born in Litchfield, Conn., June 14, 1812. Her father was the famous clergyman, Dr. Lyman Beecher, and one of her brothers was the still more famous Henry Ward Beecher. Indeed, all her many brothers and sisters were of conspicuous ability, and the family was one of the most remarkable in the history of the world.

When a young woman, Harriet Beecher studied and taught in her sister Catherine's school in Hartford. In 1832 she went to Cincinnati with her father, who had become president of Lane Theological Seminary, and there she married a member of the Seminary's teaching force, Prof. Calvin E. Stowe, a man of great ability. While in Cincinnati she often visited the slave States, gained a thorough knowledge of conditions there, and witnessed the escapes of many slaves to Canada, in which her family aided.

Two removals followed, as her husband became professor first in Bowdoin College and then in Andover Theological Seminary. She died in Hartford, July 1, 1896.

Mrs. Stowe's great work, " Uncle Tom's Cabin,"

was almost her first. It was published as a serial in the Washington *National Era* in 1851 and 1852, and in the latter year it appeared as a book, reaching, by the end of the year, on both sides of the water, the sale of more than a million copies. No other book, except Dr. Sheldon's " In His Steps," has ever won such a success. It has been translated into more than twenty languages, and it had a powerful influence in bringing about the Civil War.

Mrs. Stowe was an industrious writer, and her books enter the fields of romance, biography, essays, travel, and poetry. Her one volume of verse, " Religious Poems," was published in 1865.

She was introduced as a hymn-writer by Henry Ward Beecher, who included three of her hymns in the " Plymouth Collection," which he edited in 1855. Those three were " That mystic word of Thine, O sovereign Lord !" " When winds are raging o'er the upper ocean," and " Still, still with Thee." Mr. Sankey's famous song, " Knocking, knocking, who is there ? " was adapted from another piece in that book.

The title of the hymn we print below was first given as " Resting in God." It is based upon the words in Ps. 139 : 18 : " When I awake, I am still with thee." I give the entire hymn of six stanzas, though the third and fifth are often omitted.

Still, still with Thee, when purple morning breaketh,
  When the bird waketh and the shadows flee ;
Fairer than morning, lovelier than the daylight,
  Dawns the sweet consciousness, *I am with Thee !*

Alone with Thee ! amid the mystic shadows,
  The solemn hush of nature newly born ;
Alone with Thee in breathless adoration,
  In the calm dew and freshness of the morn.

As in the dawning, o'er the waveless ocean,
  The image of the morning star doth rest,
So, in this stillness, Thou beholdest only
  Thine image in the waters of my breast.

Still, still with Thee !　As to each new-born morning
  A fresh and solemn splendor still is given,
So doth this blessed consciousness, awaking,
  Breathe each new day nearness to Thee and heaven.

When sinks the soul, subdued by toil, to slumber,
  Its closing eye looks up to Thee in prayer,
Sweet the repose beneath Thy wings o'ershading,
  But sweeter still to wake and find Thee there.

So shall it be at last, in that bright morning,
  When the soul waketh, and life's shadows flee ;
Oh ! in that hour, fairer than daylight dawning,
  Shall rise the glorious thought—*I am with Thee.*

"Come, Ye Thankful People, Come"
Henry Alford

ONE of the finest of harvest hymns is that written by Dean Alford, "Come, ye thankful people, come."

Henry Alford was born in London, October 7, 1810. His father was a clergyman of the Church of England, and he followed in his father's footsteps. When the lad was sixteen years old, he wrote these noble words upon the fly-leaf of his Bible: "I do this day, in the presence of God and my own soul, renew my covenant with God, and solemnly determine henceforth to become His, and to do His work as far as in me lies."

He was graduated from Trinity College, Cambridge University, and became a popular London preacher. In 1857 he was promoted to the position of dean of Canterbury, and held that important post till his death fourteen years later, January 12, 1871.

Dean Alford's greatest work was a magnificent edition of the Greek Testament. He spent upon it twenty years of hard labor, and produced a work which was the admiration of scholars. He wrote many hymns. Indeed, he prepared a hymn-book to which he contributed no fewer than fifty-five hymns of his own. Not many of his hymns, however, have come into common use. Of these, one of the finest is " Ten thousand times ten thousand." Another is " Forward be our watchword." But of all his hymns the most popular is " Come, ye thankful people, come."

This harvest hymn first appeared in 1844, with the title, " After Harvest." It was originally accompanied by the text, " He that goeth forth and weepeth, bearing precious seed, shall doubtless come again with rejoicing, bringing his sheaves with him" (Ps. 126 : 6). The hymn originally contained seven stanzas, but only the following four are printed in our hymn-books :—

> Come, ye thankful people, come,
> Raise the song of Harvest-Home !
> All is safely gathered in,
> Ere the winter storms begin :
> God, our Maker, doth provide
> For our wants to be supplied ;
> Come to God's own temple, come,
> Raise the song of Harvest-Home !
>
> All the world is God's own field,
> Fruit unto His praise to yield ;
> Wheat and tares together sown,
> Unto joy or sorrow grown :
> First the blade, and then the ear,
> Then the full corn shall appear :
> Lord of harvest, grant that we
> Wholesome grain and pure may be.
>
> For the Lord our God shall come,
> And shall take His harvest home ;
> From His field shall in that day
> All offences purge away ;

Give His angels charge at last
In the fire the tares to cast,
But the fruitful ears to store
In His garner evermore.

Even so, Lord, quickly come
To Thy final Harvest-Home!
Gather Thou Thy people in,
Free from sorrow, free from sin;
There for ever purified,
In Thy presence to abide:
Come, with all Thine angels, come,
Raise the glorious Harvest-Home!

" Softly Now the Light of Day "
George Washington Doane

THE writer of this beautiful evening hymn was George Washington Doane, who was born in Trenton, N. J., May 27, 1799, and died in Burlington, N. J., April 27, 1859. After graduating from Union College he became assistant in Trinity Church, New York, then professor of rhetoric and belles-lettres in Trinity College, Hartford, and then rector of Trinity Church, Boston, the church afterward made so famous by Phillips Brooks. In 1832 he was made bishop of New Jersey, and became one of the leading bishops of the Episcopal Church. Among his works was the founding of Burlington College, and the popularizing in America of Keble's "Christian Year." His son was the eminent William C. Doane, D. D., Bishop of Albany.

Bishop Doane's volume of poems, issued in 1824, is called " Songs by the Way," and contains many poems of great beauty and power, among them the hymn printed below, and also the noble hymn, " Thou art the way; to Thee alone." Another great hymn by Bishop Doane is " Fling out the banner; let it float," one of the finest of our missionary hymns. Bishop Doane also wrote the very popular song, " What is it, mother? The lark, my child."

Here is the famous evening hymn :—

> Softly now the light of day
> Fades upon my sight away;
> Free from care, from labor free,
> Lord, I would commune with Thee.
>
> Thou, whose all-pervading eye
> Naught escapes, without, within,
> Pardon each infirmity,
> Open fault, and secret sin.
>
> Soon, for me, the light of day
> Shall forever pass away;
> Then, from sin and sorrow free,
> Take me, Lord, to dwell with Thee.
>
> Thou who, sinless, yet hast known
> All of man's infirmity,
> Then from Thine eternal throne,
> Jesus, look with pitying eye.

" Lord! While for All Mankind We Pray "
John Reynell Wreford

THIS noble, patriotic hymn was written by an English Presbyterian clergyman, Rev. John Reynell Wreford, D. D.   He was born at Barnstable in Devonshire, England, December 12, 1800, and was educated at Manchester College in York.   He became a preacher in Birmingham, but after five years' service he lost his voice to such an extent that he had to leave the ministry and become a teacher.   He died in London, July 2, 1881.

Dr. Wreford wrote many hymns, but the one before us is by far the best-known and the most widely used.   About the time of Queen Victoria's coronation, in 1837, it was composed as a national hymn and was published that year in a volume of poems which he called " Lays of Loyalty."   The hymn went at once into the hymn-books, both in England and in America, and is still a great favorite. Here are its five stanzas :—

> Lord ! while for all mankind we pray,
>   Of every clime and coast,
> Oh, hear us for our native land,
>   The land we love the most.
>
> Oh, guard our shores from every foe,
>   With peace our borders bless,
> With prosperous times our cities crown,
>   Our fields with plenteousness.

Unite us in the sacred love
   Of knowledge, truth, and Thee,
And let our hills and valleys shout
   The songs of liberty.

Here may religion, pure and mild,
   Smile on our Sabbath hours ;
And piety and virtue bless
   The home of us and ours.

Lord of the nations, thus to Thee
   Our country we commend ;
Be Thou her refuge and her trust,
   Her everlasting friend.

" Come, Ye Disconsolate "
Thomas Moore

THOMAS MOORE, who wrote the beautiful hymn we are to study, was one of the strangest of all men to write hymns. He was an Irishman, a Roman Catholic, born in Dublin, May 28, 1779. He was educated at Trinity College, Dublin, and started to study law in London, but his poetical success decided him to make literature his life-work. This he did, with one exception. In 1804 he went to Bermuda as a government official, but the work was very distasteful to him, so he put it into the hands of a deputy, traveled in America, and returned to England. The deputy, however, ran away with the proceeds of a ship and cargo, and Moore was legally liable for thirty thousand dollars!

The poet was a little man, but he was full of courage. At one time when Jeffrey, the famous critic, was harsh with his poems, Moore challenged him to a duel. The police broke in just in time, and it was discovered that one of the pistols had no bullet in it! Jeffrey and Moore became fast friends. Byron wrote in ridicule of this duel, and Moore sent him a challenge, but no duel followed, and the two poets became life-long friends. Such results certainly do not usually follow from challenges to duels!

Moore's poems became immensely popular, and

the poet received prices for them that were far in excess of what had ever before been paid for literary work. His long poem, " Lalla Rookh," brought him $15,000 before a copy was sold. Among his other popular works were his " Irish Melodies," his " National Airs," and his " Ballads and Songs," containing such famous pieces as " Go Where Glory Waits Thee," " The Harp That Once Through Tara's Halls," " Believe Me, if All These Endearing Young Charms," " The Last Rose of Summer," " Those Evening Bells," and " Oft in the Stilly Night."

Moore was a good son, and a loving husband to his admirable wife. He was a warm and true friend. The last three years of his life were sad ones, for he lost his mental powers and required his wife's constant care. He died in his seventy-third year, February 26, 1852.

He wrote thirty-two hymns, all contained in one collection of " Sacred Songs," which were published in 1816. In this set of poems are some that have become very famous : " This World is All a Fleeting Show," " The Bird Let Loose in Eastern Skies," " Sound the Loud Timbrel o'er Egypt's Dark Sea," and " Thou Art, O God, the Life and Light." Among the greatest of these favorites is the hymn, " Come, Ye Disconsolate." Here is the way Moore wrote it :—

Come, ye disconsolate, where'er ye languish ;
   Come, at the shrine of God fervently kneel ;
Here bring your wounded hearts ; here tell your anguish —
   Earth has no sorrow that heaven cannot heal.

Joy of the desolate, light of the straying,
  Hope, when all others die, fadeless and pure ;
Here speaks the Comforter, in God's name saying,
  "Earth has no sorrow that heaven cannot cure."

Come, ask the infidel what boon he brings us,
  What charm for aching hearts he can reveal,
Sweet is that heavenly promise Hope sings us —
  "Earth has no sorrow that God cannot heal."

Dr. Thomas Hastings changed the second line of the first stanza to read, " Come to the mercy-seat, fervently kneel." The second stanza he changed to read :—

Joy of the comfortless, light of the straying,
  Hope of the penitent, fadeless and pure ;
Here speaks the Comforter, tenderly saying,
  "Earth has no sorrow that heaven cannot cure."

The third stanza was so changed by Dr. Hastings as hardly to be recognized :—

Here see the bread of life ; see waters flowing
  Forth from the throne of God, pure from above ;
Come to the feast of love ; come, ever knowing
  Earth hath no sorrow but heaven can remove.

These changes introduced by Dr. Hastings are to be found in all our hymn-books. Some of them are improvements, some are the reverse ; but as a whole the hymn has gained in singing qualities and in thought because of them.

"Oh, Worship the King, All-glorious Above"
Robert Grant

SIR ROBERT GRANT, who wrote this hymn, was born in the county of Inverness, Scotland, in 1785, and his father was at one time a member of Parliament and a director of the famous East India Company. The boy followed in his father's footsteps, for, after an education at Cambridge University, he himself became, in 1826, member of Parliament for Inverness, and in 1834 he became governor of Bombay. He died at Dapoorie in western India, July 9, 1838. It was in India that he wrote his two books on that country, and other works. It is of interest that, while he was a member of Parliament, the historian, Macaulay, made his first speech in Parliament in support of Sir Robert Grant's bill for giving some of their rights to the Jews.

Sir Robert wrote twelve hymns and other poems, which were published in a little book, after his death, by his brother Charles. Of these the most famous and beautiful is the one we have chosen ; but another noble hymn by Sir Robert Grant is, "When gathering clouds around I view," and another begins,

" Saviour ! when in dust to Thee
Low we bow the adoring knee."

"Oh, worship the King, all-glorious above," is a versification of Psalm 104. Only four stanzas are usually sung, but we give six : —

Oh, worship the King, all-glorious above ;
Oh, gratefully sing His power and His love ;
Our shield and defender, the Ancient of Days,
Pavilioned in splendor, and girded with praise.

Oh, tell of His might, oh, sing of His grace !
Whose robe is the light, whose canopy, space.
His chariots of wrath the deep thunder-clouds form,
And dark is His path on the wings of the storm.

The earth, with its store of wonders untold,
Almighty, Thy power hath founded of old ;
Hath 'stablished it fast by a changeless decree,
And round it hath cast, like a mantle, the sea.

Thy bountiful care what tongue can recite ?
It breathes in the air, it shines in the light,
It streams from the hills, it descends to the plain,
And sweetly distils in the dew and the rain.

Frail children of dust, and feeble as frail,
In Thee do we trust, nor find Thee to fail.
Thy mercies how tender ! how firm to the end !
Our maker, defender, Redeemer, and friend !

O measureless Might ! ineffable Love !
While angels delight to hymn Thee above,
The humbler creation, though feeble their lays,
With true adoration shall lisp to Thy praise.

"We Thank Thee, Lord, for This Fair Earth"

George Edward Lynch Cotton

THIS beautiful Thanksgiving hymn was written by George Edward Lynch Cotton, D. D., an English clergyman, and it is the only one of his hymns that has come into common use.

He was born at Chester, England, October 29, 1813. His father, Captain Thomas Cotton, was killed in war on November 13 of the same year.

Young Cotton was educated at the Cambridge University, Trinity College, and graduated in 1836. At once he became assistant master in the famous school of Rugby, where Tom Brown of the well-known story went to school.

In 1852 he became head master of Marlborough College. In 1858 he was made Bishop of Calcutta, succeeding Dr. Daniel Wilson in this post made famous by the life of the consecrated Bishop Heber, who wrote so many beautiful hymns.

Bishop Cotton's life came to a tragic end on October 6, 1866. He was drowned at Koshtea while disembarking from a steamer.

This Thanksgiving hymn was published in 1856 in "Hymns for Use in the Chapel of Marlborough College," and appeared in four stanzas of four lines each, as follows : —

We thank Thee, Lord, for this fair earth,
    The glittering sky, the silver sea;
For all their beauty, all their worth,
    Their light and glory, come from Thee.

Thine are the flowers that clothe the ground,
    The trees that wave their arms above,
The hills that gird our dwellings round,
    As Thou dost gird Thine own with love.

Yet teach us still how far more fair,
    Thou glorious Father, in Thy sight
Is one pure deed, one holy prayer,
    One heart that owns Thy Spirit's might.

So while we gaze with thoughtful eye
    On all the gifts Thy love has given,
Help us in Thee to live and die,
    By Thee to rise from earth to heaven.

"Once in Royal David's City"
Cecil Frances Alexander

THIS is one of the most beautiful of Christmas hymns. It was written by Mrs. Cecil Frances Alexander, who was born in County Tyrone, Ireland, in 1823. Her father was Major John Humphreys. In 1850 she was married to Rt. Rev. William Alexander, Bishop of Derry and Raphoe, now Archbishop of Armagh and Primate of all Ireland.

Mrs. Alexander wrote nearly four hundred hymns and poems, contained in more than eight volumes. Nearly all of her hymns were written for children. As would be suited to her audience, her hymns are exceedingly simple in their language, and yet she treats, and treats adequately, the most profound truths of religion.

Her most famous religious poem is " The Burial of Moses," a very noble picture of that mysterious scene. Among her hymns the best known is " There is a green hill far away." Another famous hymn from her pen is "Jesus calls us o'er the tumult." Another begins with the line, " All things bright and beautiful."

The Christmas hymn, "Once in royal David's city," was printed in 1848 as a part of the volume, " Hymns for Little Children." It is as follows : —

Once in royal David's city
 Stood a lowly cattle-shed,
Where a mother laid her baby
 In a manger for His bed:
Mary was that mother mild,
Jesus Christ her little child.

He came down to earth from heaven
 Who is God and Lord of all,
And His shelter was a stable,
 And His cradle was a stall;
With the lowly, poor, and mean,
Lived on earth our Saviour then.

And, through all His wondrous childhood,
 He would honor and obey,
Love and watch the lowly maiden
 In whose gentle arms He lay:
Christian children all must be
Mild, obedient, good as He.

Oh, our eyes at last shall see Him,
 Through His own redeeming love,
For that child so dear and gentle
 Is our God in heaven above;
And He leads His children on
To the place where He is gone.

Not in that poor lowly stable,
 With the oxen standing by,
We shall see Him; but in heaven,
 Set at God's right hand on high;
When like stars His children crowned
All in white shall wait around.

" While Shepherds Watched Their Flocks by Night "

Nahum Tate

NAHUM TATE, who wrote this hymn, was the son of Faithful Tate, an Irish clergyman, who himself was a little of a poet. Our hymn-writer was born in Dublin in 1652, became a friend and literary associate of the great poet Dryden, and succeeded Shadwell as poet-laureate of England, a post to which he was appointed by King William III. Among his poems are a birthday ode for George I. He is said to have been a drunkard and a spendthrift. He died as an officer of the Royal Mint, in London, 1715.

Before Tate's day, for a century and a half, the English churches had been singing a very inferior version of the Psalms by Sternhold and Hopkins. With his friend, Dr. Nicholas Brady, another Irishman, Nahum Tate wrote a version of the Psalms which obtained royal favor, and was finally, though after some opposition, adopted by the churches and known as the " new version." It was published in 1696, and the hymns it contains, so far as they are still in use, must be referred to as by " Tate and Brady," since it is not known who wrote the individual pieces.

In 1703, however, a supplement was published

which is known to have been written by Tate. This
supplement contained the famous Christmas hymn:—

>While shepherds watched their flocks by night,
> All seated on the ground,
>The angel of the Lord came down,
> And glory shone around.
>" Fear not," said he—for mighty dread
> Had seized their troubled mind —
>" Glad tidings of great joy I bring,
> To you and all mankind.

>" To you, in David's town this day,
> Is born of David's line
>The Saviour, who is Christ, the Lord,
> And this shall be the sign : —
>The heavenly babe you there shall find
> To human view displayed,
>All meanly wrapped in swathing bands,
> And in a manger laid."

>Thus spake the seraph—and forthwith
> Appeared a shining throng
>Of angels, praising God, who thus
> Addressed their joyful song:
>" All glory be to God on high,
> And to the earth be peace ;
>Good-will henceforth from heaven to men
> Begin, and never cease ! "

"Great God! We Sing Thy Mighty Hand."
Philip Doddridge

THIS hymn is by one of the very greatest of English hymn-writers, Rev. Philip Doddridge, D. D., who was born in London, June 26, 1702. His father was an oil-merchant. Philip was the last of twenty children, and at his birth he was so feeble that he was given up to die; indeed, all through his life his health was very delicate. Both of his parents were pious people, and his mother used to teach him Bible history from some Dutch tiles that were on the walls of her room.

The lad was left an orphan while he was quite young, but kind friends cared for him and sent him to school. He learned so well that the Duchess of Bedford became interested in him, and offered to send him to either Oxford or Cambridge University, provided he would become a clergyman of the Church of England; but his grandfather had been an Independent or Congregationalist, and his parents had belonged to the same church, so that the boy refused the offer, and was educated at a seminary of the church of his choice.

His thoughts naturally turned to the ministry, and he preached his first sermon at the age of twenty. After a pastorate at Kibworth he became, in 1729, the minister of a church in Northampton, where he preached for twenty years. He was also the head of a theological seminary there, teaching a great variety of subjects, and preparing scores of young men for the ministry.

Toward the end of 1750 it became evident that consumption had set in. A voyage to Lisbon was suggested, but Dr. Doddridge was too poor for that. A friend of his, a clergyman of the Church of England, thereupon got up a subscription, and speedily raised for this purpose $1,500, for the graces of Doddridge's character made him greatly beloved by men of all classes and beliefs. Doddridge went to Lisbon, but his disease carried him off the next year, and on October 26, 1751, he went to join the singing hosts of heaven.

Doddridge's hymns were nearly all based upon Scripture, and many of them repeat the Bible thoughts and phrases with much fidelity. They were written for his sermons, and were lined off to the congregation at the close of the service. During Dr. Doddridge's lifetime they were circulated in manuscript, and were not printed till 1755, when a collection of them was put forth by his friend, Job Orton.

Doddridge wrote more than four hundred hymns, a large number of which are still in use. He was an imitator of his friend, Dr. Watts, but was a more even writer, not rising so high as Watts, nor sinking so near to the level of prose. He wrote many valuable prose works, the most famous being his commentary on the New Testament, " The Family Expositor," and his " Rise and Progress of Religion

in the Soul." His best-known hymns are : " Jesus !
I love Thy charming name," " Awake, my soul,
stretch every nerve," " Do I not love Thee, O my
Lord ? " " Grace, 'tis a charming sound," " Triumphant Zion, lift thy head," " O God of Bethel by
whose hand," and " O happy day that fixed my
choice."

The new-year's hymn that we have chosen was
published with the heading, " Help obtained of God,
Acts 26 : 22." Several lines appear in different
forms ; I give the version that seems to me the
best : —

> Great God ! we sing Thy mighty hand
> By which supported still we stand ;
> The opening year Thy mercy shows ;
> Let mercy crown it till it close.
>
> By day, by night, at home, abroad,
> Still we are guarded by our God ;
> By His incessant bounty fed,
> By His unerring counsel led.
>
> With grateful hearts the past we own ;
> The future, all to us unknown,
> We to Thy guardian care commit,
> And peaceful leave before Thy feet.
>
> In scenes exalted or depressed,
> Be Thou our joy and Thou our rest ;
> Thy goodness all our hopes shall raise,
> Adored through all our changing days.
>
> When death shall interrupt our songs,
> And seal in silence mortal tongues,
> Our Helper, God, in whom we trust,
> In better worlds our souls shall boast.

"Father, I Know That All My Life"
Anna Laetitia Waring

VERY little is known about the author of this hymn, because of her remarkably retiring disposition. She was Miss Anna Laetitia Waring, and was born in Neath, a town of South Wales, in 1820. In 1850 she published her " Hymns and Meditations," and in 1858 she published " Additional Hymns." It is believed that she was a Friend, and that her life was full of suffering and pain.

Miss Waring's hymns are beautiful in every way, and two of them have become world-favorites—the one printed below, and " In Heavenly Love Abiding." " Father, I Know That All My Life " was included in Miss Waring's first volume of poems, and there it was given the title, " My Times Are in Thy Hand." It had originally eight stanzas of six lines each, and I give it below in the longer form ; but in singing, the first five stanzas are all that are usually used. In our hymn-books, also, many of the lines are shortened to make the rhythm smoother. Here is the hymn, just as Miss Waring wrote it :—

> Father, I know that all my life
>   Is portioned out for me,
> And the changes that are sure to come
>   I do not fear to see ;
> But I ask Thee for a present mind
>   Intent on pleasing Thee.

270

I ask Thee for a thoughtful love,
  Through constant watching wise,
To meet the glad with joyful smiles,
  And to wipe the weeping eyes ;
And a heart at leisure from itself,
  To soothe and sympathize.

I would not have the restless will
  That hurries to and fro,
Seeking for some great thing to do
  Or secret thing to know ;
I would be treated as a child,
  And guided where I go.

Wherever in the world I am,
  In whatsoe'er estate,
I have a fellowship with hearts
  To keep and cultivate ;
And a work of lowly love to do
  For the Lord on whom I wait.

So I ask Thee for the daily strength,
  To none that ask denied,
And a mind to blend with outward life
  While keeping at Thy side ;
Content to fill a little space,
  If Thou be glorified.

And if some things I do not ask
  In my cup of blessing be,
I would have my spirit filled the more
  With grateful love to Thee,
More careful, not to serve Thee much,
  But to please Thee perfectly.

There are briers besetting every path
  That call for patient care ;
There is a cross in every lot,
  And an earnest need for prayer ;
But a lowly heart that leans on Thee
  Is happy anywhere.

In a service which Thy will appoints
  There are no bonds for me ;
For my inmost heart is taught " the truth "
  That makes Thy children " free " ·
And a life of self-renouncing love
  Is a life of liberty.

"O, Where Are Kings and Empires Now?"
Arthur Cleveland Coxe

THIS hymn was written by a distinguished bishop of the American Episcopal Church, the Rt. Rev. Arthur Cleveland Coxe. He was born in Mendham, N. J., May 10, 1818, and died in 1896. His father, Rev. Samuel H. Cox, D. D., was a famous Presbyterian clergyman, and father and son carried on for many years a very earnest but good-natured discussion, not only over the son's departure from the father's denomination, but over his adding an "e" to the end of his name!

The young man graduated from the University of New York in 1838, and after successful pastorates in Hartford, Baltimore, and New York City, he became, in 1865, bishop of Western New York, having previously been chosen bishop of Texas, but declining.

Most of Bishop Coxe's poems were composed in his youth, and his most famous book, "Christian Ballads," was published in 1840. Among his most notable hymns are "We are living, we are dwelling in a grand and awful time," "Saviour, sprinkle many nations," "In the silent midnight watches," and the hymn here chosen, "O, Where Are Kings and Empires Now?" Though Bishop Coxe's hymns were speedily adopted by every other denomination,

273

he was himself a member of the Episcopal committee on the selection of hymns, and his modesty kept
his own work out of the hymnal of his own church.

" O, Where Are Kings and Empires Now ? " was
originally published in *The Churchman* in 1839, and
was included in " Christian Ballads " in 1840. Its
four stanzas are a condensation of ten double stanzas.

On one occasion a powerful impression was produced by a stanza of the hymn. It was at the general conference of the Evangelical Alliance in 1873,
in New York City. President Woolsey of Yale was
speaking on the scepticism regarding prayer that
was so common at that time. At length with great
force he quoted :—

> " O, where are kings and empires now,
> Of old that went and came ?
> But, Lord, Thy church is praying *yet*,
> A thousand years the same ! "

The entire assembly burst into applause, and many
eyes were wet with the depth of feeling.

Here is the hymn, in the short form used in all the
hymn-books :—

> O, where are kings and empires now,
> Of old that went and came ?
> But, Lord, Thy church is praying yet,
> A thousand years the same.
>
> We mark her goodly battlements,
> And her foundations strong ;
> We hear within the solemn voice
> Of her unending song.

For not like kingdoms of the world
  Thy holy church, O God !
Though earthquake's shocks are threatening her,
  And tempests are abroad,—

Unshaken as eternal hills,
  Immovable she stands,
A mountain that shall fill the earth,
  A house not made by hands.

"Come, Said Jesus' Sacred Voice"
Anna Laetitia Barbauld

ANNA LAETITIA AIKIN was a wonderful little girl. She was born in Leicestershire, England, June 20, 1743. Her father was Rev. John Aikin, D. D., a Presbyterian minister who became a school-teacher. Before the girl was two years old she could read sentences and short stories without spelling her words, and in half a year afterward she could read as well as most women. When she was five years old, her father was talking one day with a friend about the condition of the angels in heaven, and was remarking that, since joy meant additional happiness, they could not experience joy, because they were perfectly happy already. "I think you are mistaken, papa," Anna piped up, "because in the chapter I read to you this morning from the New Testament, it said that there is more joy in heaven over one sinner that repenteth than over ninety and nine persons that need no repentance." The gifted child soon became acquainted with many of the best English authors, and by the time she reached the age of twenty she had become familiar with French and Italian, besides learning a great deal of Latin and Greek.

But Anna Aikin's life was a very sad one, because of an unhappy marriage. In 1774 she was wedded to Rev. Rochemont Barbauld, a Unitarian minister, who also, like Dr. Aikin, became a school-teacher. Mrs. Barbauld was his assistant in his school. He was a man of very violent temper, which in time developed into insanity. He attacked Mrs. Barbauld with a knife, and she was obliged to put him into an asylum. He escaped, and committed suicide by drowning in 1808. Mrs. Barbauld continued to live in her husband's home, and reached a good old age, dying on March 9, 1825, greatly honored by all.

Mrs. Barbauld wrote twenty-one hymns, the most famous being "Awake, my soul! lift up thine eyes," "Again the Lord of life and light," "How blest the righteous when he dies," and "Praise to God, immortal praise." The hymn we have chosen is entitled "The Gracious Call." It was written about 1792, and is based, of course, upon Matt. 11 : 28, "Come unto me, and I will give you rest." It consists of four stanzas :—

> Come, said Jesus' sacred voice,
> Come, and make my path your choice ;
> I will guide you to your home ;
> Weary pilgrim, hither come.
>
> Thou who, houseless, sole, forlorn,
> Long hast borne the proud world's scorn,
> Long hast roamed the barren waste,
> Weary pilgrim, hither haste.
>
> Ye who, tossed on beds of pain,
> Seek for ease, but seek in vain ;
> Ye by fiercer anguish torn,
> In remorse for guilt who mourn ;

> Hither come, for here is found
> Balm that flows for every wound !
> Peace that ever shall endure,
> Rest eternal, sacred, sure.

Probably the most famous bit of writing done by Mrs. Barbauld are the following lines, from a short poem written about twelve years before her death:—

> Life ! we've been long together,
> Through pleasant and through cloudy weather.
> 'Tis hard to part when friends are dear —
> Perhaps 'twill cost a sigh, a tear.
> Then steal away; give little warning;
> Choose thine own time;
> Say not good-night,—but in some brighter clime
> Bid me good-morning !

" That Sweet Story of Old "
Jemima Luke

THERE died, in 1906, in the Isle of Wight, Mrs. Jemima Luke, the beloved author of that world-famous song for children (and adults, too, for that matter), "I think when I read that sweet story of old."

Mrs. Luke was 92 years old when she passed away. Her famous song was written 65 years before, in 1841. At that time she was Miss Jemima Thompson, the daughter of a missionary enthusiast, and herself a whole-souled laborer for the Lord.

One day she was driving out to see to some work in which she was interested, and, as the journey was an hour long, she occupied her time composing the hymn. The last two stanzas, "But thousands and thousands who wander and fall," were added as an afterthought, to fit the song for use in missionary gatherings. The song was first sung soon after at Blagdon School, where Miss Thompson herself taught it to the children.

Though the gifted author wrote much, no other poem of hers has so seized upon popular fancy. Of this hymn, however, she continued to hear up to the last, and from all parts of the world messages of gratitude were constantly coming to her.

She herself was very modest, and insisted that she was over-praised. Her character was a very charming one, and she was widely beloved. She was accepted as a missionary to the women of India, and was on the point of setting out when a failure of her health compelled her to abandon that design. She edited *The Missionary Repository*, the first missionary magazine for children, which numbered among its contributors David Livingstone, Robert Moffat, and James Montgomery. The last years of her life were largely devoted to the very important work of building parsonages for communities not able to provide them for themselves. In 1843 she married Rev. Samuel Luke, of Bristol, and for 25 years, until he died, she was a model pastor's wife.

Mrs. Luke and Christian Endeavorers came together on several notable occasions. The inimitable musical director of the splendid London Convention of 1900 was Rev. Carey Bonner, general secretary of the British Sunday School Union. He wrote for that Convention a new setting of " I think when I read that sweet story of old," and it was sung at the Junior rally by 1,200 Juniors. Mrs. Luke was not well enough to be present, but she sent a letter to the children, which was read to them by another famous poet, Marianne Farningham.

This music Mrs. Luke wanted to hear, so copies of it were sent to half a dozen children in Newport, her home on the Isle of Wight, and they, with Mr. Bonner, sung it to her.

Again, at the Baltimore Christian Endeavor Convention, where Mr. Bonner was the musical director, the hymn was sung as part of the magnificent "Festival of Praise," and Mrs. Luke wrote for the occasion a delightful message, which was printed in facsimile, and distributed through the audience. Some sentences from that message may well be taken as summing up her beautiful life :—

"Dear children, you will be men and women soon, and it is for you and the children of England to carry the message of a Saviour's love to every nation of this sin-stricken world. It is a blessed message to carry, and it is happy work to do. The Lord make you ever faithful to Him, and unspeakably happy in His service! I came to Him at ten years of age, and at ninety-one can testify to His care and faithfulness."

The following is the entire hymn : —

I think when I read that sweet story of old,
   When Jesus was here among men,
How He called little children as lambs to His fold,
   I should like to have been with them then.

I wish that His hands had been placed on my head,
   That His arm had been thrown around me,
And that I might have seen His kind look when
     He said,
   " Let the little ones come unto me."

Yet still to His footstool in prayer I may go,
   And ask for a share in His love ;
And if I thus earnestly seek Him below,
   I shall see Him and hear Him above,

In that beautiful place He has gone to prepare
  For all who are washed and forgiven;
And many dear children shall be with Him there,
  For of such is the kingdom of heaven.

But thousands and thousands who wander and fall
  Never heard of that heavenly home;
I wish they could know there is room for them all,
  And that Jesus had bid them to come.

I long for the joy of that glorious time,
  The sweetest, the brightest, the best;
When the dear little children of every clime
  Shall crowd to His arms and be blest.

" The Star-Spangled Banner "
Francis Scott Key

THIS song is not a hymn, strictly speaking, but it is one of our national anthems.

The father of Francis Scott Key was a Revolutionary patriot, whose boy was born at Frederick, Md., August 1, 1779. The lad was educated at St. John's College, Annapolis, and became a brilliant lawyer. He practised in Washington, and was United States district attorney there for three terms, holding that office at his death.

Mr. Key wrote a number of hymns, one of which, "Lord, with glowing heart I'd praise Thee," is still very widely used. His most famous production, however, is of course that stirring patriotic anthem, "The Star-Spangled Banner."

It was written during the war of 1812. On August 14, 1814, Key went from Baltimore to visit the British fleet at the mouth of the Potomac, in order to obtain the release of a friend who had been captured. But an attack on Baltimore was about to be made, so that Mr. Key, with his truce-boat, was detained all night, while the bombardment of Fort McHenry, in the harbor of Baltimore, was vigorously carried on.

It was a night of deep anxiety. "Just before day the cannonading ceased. Key, and his friend who had gone with him, paced the deck until dawn, eager for the first streak of day to disclose the result. With 'the dawn's early light' they caught sight of 'the broad stripes and bright stars' of the dear old flag still floating over the fort."

Key was successful in his mission, and as he went back to the city he hastily wrote, on the back of a letter, the first draft of "The Star-Spangled Banner." It was at once completed, and that same day was printed and circulated all over Baltimore. It became popular instantly, being sung to the same tune that is still used,—the tune of "Anacreon in Heaven."

The bronze statue of Key, placed in 1898 over his grave at Frederick, Md., shows him with his hand outstretched, as at the moment when he discovered that "our flag was still there," while his other arm is waving his hat exultantly.

It is good to know that Mr. Key was a man of fine Christian character. He was kindly in his personal relations, charitable, the earnest friend of the colored men, fervent in public prayer, and a very active member of the Protestant Episcopal Church. He was just such a man as we would have chosen to write our national anthem. And here are the words : —

Oh ! say, can you see by the dawn's early light
What so proudly we hailed at the twilight's last gleaming,—
Whose broad stripes and bright stars through the perilous
    fight,
O'er the ramparts we watched, were so gallantly streaming ?

And the rocket's red glare, the bombs bursting in air,
Gave proof through the night that our flag was still there;
Oh! say, does that star-spangled banner yet wave
O'er the land of the free, and the home of the brave?

On that shore, dimly seen through the mists of the deep,
Where the foe's haughty host in dread silence reposes,
What is that which the breeze, o'er the towering steep,
As it fitfully blows, now conceals, now discloses?
Now it catches the gleam of the morning's first beam,
In full glory reflected now shines on the stream;
'Tis the star-spangled banner; oh, long may it wave
O'er the land of the free, and the home of the brave!

And where is that band who so vauntingly swore
That the havoc of war and the battle's confusion
A home and a country should leave us no more?
Their blood has washed out their foul footsteps' pollution.
No refuge could save the hireling and slave
From the terror of flight, or the gloom of the grave;
And the star-spangled banner in triumph doth wave
O'er the land of the free, and the home of the brave.

Oh! thus be it ever, when freemen shall stand
Between their loved homes and the war's desolation!
Blest with victory and peace, may the heaven-rescued land
Praise the Power that hath made and preserved us a nation.
Then conquer we must, when our cause it is just;
And this be our motto, "In God is our trust";
And the star-spangled banner in triumph shall wave
O'er the land of the free, and the home of the brave.

"Lord of All Being, Throned Afar"

Oliver Wendell Holmes

OLIVER WENDELL HOLMES, who wrote this hymn, was one of the best beloved of American poets. He was born in Cambridge, Mass., August 29, 1809, and died in Boston, October 7, 1894. First he studied law, but turned from that to medicine, and became a distinguished professor of anatomy and physiology, first at Dartmouth and then, through the greater part of his life, at Harvard.

Dr. Holmes was a wise and witty man, and wisdom and wit are combined in his poems, essays, and novels. His first notable poem, "Old Ironsides," saved from destruction the historic frigate, Constitution. His first important literary work was the series of remarkable essays which he contributed to *The Atlantic Monthly* when it was founded,—"The Autocrat of the Breakfast-Table." A brighter set of essays was never written, and at once Dr. Holmes became a favorite writer of prose, as he was already a favorite writer of poetry.

A second series of essays followed in *The Atlantic Monthly*, entitled "The Professor at the Breakfast-Table." It was Dr. Holmes's pleasant habit to close his chapters with poems by himself. One of the poems thus used in that series was the beautiful hymn,

> " O Love Divine, that stooped to share
> Our sharpest pang, our bitterest tear."

The last chapter closed with an invitation to his readers to join him " in singing (inwardly) this hymn to the Source of the light we all need to lead us, and the warmth which alone can make us all brothers." Then followed the hymn before us, which he called " A Sunday Hymn." It was written in 1848, though the chapter of " The Professor at the Breakfast-Table " in which it appeared was printed in December, 1859. The hymn is probably the finest statement of God's omnipresence in the English language, outside of the Bible.

> Lord of all being, throned afar,
> Thy glory flames from sun and star ;
> Centre and soul of every sphere,
> Yet to each loving heart how near !
>
> Sun of our life, Thy quickening ray
> Sheds on our path the glow of day ;
> Star of our hope, Thy softened light
> Cheers the long watches of the night.
>
> Our midnight is Thy smile withdrawn ;
> Our noontide is Thy gracious dawn ;
> Our rainbow arch Thy mercy's sign :
> All, save the clouds of sin, are Thine !
>
> Lord of all life, below, above,
> Whose light is truth, whose warmth is love,
> Before Thy ever-blazing throne
> We ask no lustre of our own.

Grant us Thy truth to make us free,
And kindling hearts that burn for Thee,
Till all Thy living altars claim
One holy light, one heavenly flame !

"O God, beneath Thy Guiding Hand"
Leonard Bacon

THIS is one of the best known of American patriotic hymns. It was written by Leonard Bacon, who was born in Detroit, February 19, 1802. Detroit was then hardly more than a fort and a trading-post, and his father was a missionary there, leading the Indians in the way of life. No wonder the son always had the deepest and most active interest in missions.

Young Leonard became a student at Yale College and at Andover Theological Seminary. In 1825, almost immediately after his graduation from Andover, he became pastor of the First Congregational Church of New Haven, where he remained, as pastor and pastor emeritus, for fifty-seven years,—the rest of his life. In 1866 he became professor of theology in Yale Divinity School; but in 1871 he resigned that post and became lecturer on Church Polity. He was one of the founders of *The Independent* and *The New Englander*, and was editor of both. He was a vigorous and powerful Abolitionist, and with his strong convictions he was all his life a determined advocate of many noble causes. He died December 23, 1881.

Dr. Bacon edited several hymn-books, and wrote a number of hymns that have come into common

use.   Among these are " Wake the song of jubilee,"
" Though now the nations sit beneath the darkness
of o'erspreading death," "Hail! tranqui! hour of
closing day," and his best-known hymn, given below.
It was originally written for use in the celebration of
the second centennial of New Haven, and in it are
compressed the leading ideas of its writer's life.

> O God, beneath Thy guiding hand
>   Our exiled fathers crossed the sea,
> And when they trod the wintry strand,
>   With prayer and psalm they worshipped Thee.
>
> Thou heardst, ·well pleased, the song, the prayer ;
>   Thy blessing came ; and still its power
> Shall onward through all ages bear
>   The memory of that holy hour.
>
> What change ! through pathless wilds no more
>   The fierce and naked savage roams :
> Sweet praise, along the cultured shore,
>   Breaks from ten thousand happy homes.
>
> Laws, freedom, truth, and faith in God
>   Came with those exiles o'er the waves,
> And where their pilgrim feet have trod,
>   The God they trusted guards their graves.
>
> And here Thy name, O God of love,
>   Their children's children shall adore,
> Till these eternal hills remove
>   And spring adorns the earth no more.

"Tell Me the Old, Old Story"
Katherine Hankey

THIS simple but beautiful song was written by an English woman, Miss Katherine Hankey, the daughter of a banker in London. In 1866 Miss Hankey wrote a poem of fifty stanzas. It was about the life of Jesus, and was in two parts, the first being entitled, "The Story Wanted," and the second, "The Story Told." From the first part two well-known hymns have been taken,—the one we have selected for printing here, and the companion hymn, that is often printed alongside in our hymn-books, "I love to tell the story."

Miss Hankey was recovering from a serious illness when she wrote "Tell me the old, old story," and the line, "For I am weak and weary," was only a picture of her condition at the time. The poem was begun in January, but it was not finished till November of that year.

Here is the way the song, "Tell me the old, old story," came to be set to music.

Dr. Doane, the well-known composer, attended in 1867, the year after the poem was written, an international convention of the Young Men's Christian Associations, held in Montreal. In the audience of Christian workers was Major-General Russell, who was particularly noted just then because of popular excitement over the question of Ireland, leading to many riots, and General Russell was in charge of the British troops.

In the course of one of the meetings, when a great crowd was present, General Russell rose, and read Miss Hankey's beautiful poem. He was profoundly moved, and the tears streamed down his cheeks. Dr. Doane was also much impressed by the hymn, and obtained a copy of the words. Then, afterward, in a stage-coach in the White Mountains, with the grand scenery all around him, he wrote the music that has since become so familiar ; and that evening the hymn, wedded now to the tune, was sung for the first time in the parlors of the Crawford House.

"Tell me the old, old story" is popular now all over the world. It has been translated into German, Spanish, Welsh, Italian, and other languages, and it is sung everywhere with equal pleasure because it expresses with such clearness the love that all Christians feel for their dear Redeemer.

Here is the hymn :—

> Tell me the old, old story,
>   Of unseen things above,
> Of Jesus and His glory,
>   Of Jesus and His love.
> Tell me the story simply,
>   As to a little child,
> For I am weak and weary,
>   And helpless and defiled.
>
> Tell me the story slowly,
>   That I may take it in —
> That wonderful redemption,
>   God's remedy for sin.

Tell me the story often,
  For I forget so soon ;
The early dew of morning
  Has passed away at noon.

Tell me the story softly,
  With earnest tones, and grave ;
Remember ! I'm the sinner
  Whom Jesus came to save.
Tell me that story always,
  If you would really be,
In any time of trouble,
  A comforter to me.

Tell me the same old story,
  When you have cause to fear
That this world's empty glory
  Is costing me too dear.
Yes, and when that world's glory
  Is dawning on my soul,
Tell me the old, old story:
  " Christ Jesus makes thee whole."

"Glorious Things of Thee Are Spoken"
John Newton

NONE of our hymn-writers has had a history so remarkable as that of John Newton, who wrote this noble hymn. He was born in London, July 24, 1725. His mother was a pious woman, who taught him the Catechism and many other good things; but she died when the lad was only six years old.

His father was a sea-captain, and could not supply the place of a mother. He took the boy to sea when he was eleven years old, and the young fellow learned to curse and blaspheme, and became very wild. After his father retired from the sea, the son made several voyages by himself. At one time he was forced into the navy, a war being expected, and he became a midshipman. But he was very restless and he deserted, was caught, stripped, whipped severely, and degraded to the ranks.

By this time he had become a thorough infidel, and was steeped in all kinds of sin. He fell into the hands of a slave-trader in Africa, and suffered all manner of hardships there, being continually insulted and almost starved. Delivered providentially from that terrible situation, after many strange and hazardous adventures he became a slave-trader himself, and made several voyages to Africa in that shameful occupation.

The reading of Thomas à Kempis, the fearful ex-

periences of a storm at sea in which his ship was almost lost, his deliverance from a severe fever in
Africa,—these, and other experiences, at last awoke
in the sinful man the memories of the religion his
mother had taught him, and he turned from his sins
with true repentance.

His conversion was so complete that he became a
minister of the gospel.   This was in 1764, when he
was thirty-nine years old.   He settled in Olney, England, and there it was that he formed the beautiful
friendship with William Cowper which has given to
the world so many splendid hymns.   Some think
that it was with the desire to draw Cowper's mind
away from his deep melancholy that Newton proposed that the two should compose a series of hymns
together.   Of the famous collection that resulted,
" The Olney Hymns," Cowper is said to have written
sixty-six, while Newton wrote the rest of the three
hundred and forty-nine.   But more of Cowper's
hymns than of Newton's have become famous.

"Safely through another week" is one of Newton's hymns that is most often sung.   Others are :
" How sweet the name of Jesus sounds," " Approach,
my soul, the mercy seat," " Come, my soul, thy suit
prepare," "For a season called to part," "Great
Shepherd of Thy ransomed flock," " In evil long I
took delight " (which surely paints his own expe-
periences), " Jesus ! who knows full well," " Lord ! I
cannot let Thee go," " One there is above all others,"
" Quiet, Lord ! my froward heart," " Saviour, visit
Thy plantation," "Sometimes a light surprises,"
"'Tis a point I long to know," " While with cease-

less course the sun," and still others that are found
in most of our hymn-books.

But the greatest of all the hymns of John Newton
is "Glorious things of thee are spoken." It is a
noble description of the people of God, under the
protection of their supreme leader. Newton wrote
five stanzas, and you will like to see all of them.
The last two, however, are inferior to the first three,
and are seldom printed in our hymn-books.

> Glorious things of thee are spoken,
>   Zion, city of our God !
> He, whose word cannot be broken,
>   Form'd thee for His own abode :
> On the Rock of ages founded,
>   What can shake thy sure repose ?
> With salvation's walls surrounded,
>   Thou may'st smile at all thy foes.
>
> See ! the streams of living waters,
>   Springing from eternal love,
> Well supply thy sons and daughters,
>   And all fear of want remove.
> Who can faint when such a river
>   Ever flows their thirst to assuage ?
> Grace, which, like the Lord, the giver,
>   Never fails from age to age.
>
> Round each habitation hov'ring,
>   See the cloud and fire appear !
> For a glory and a cov'ring,
>   Showing that the Lord is near ;
> Thus deriving, from their banner,
>   Light by night, and shade by day :
> Safe they feed upon the manna
>   Which He gives them when they pray.

Bless'd inhabitants of Zion,
   Wash'd in the Redeemer's blood !
Jesus, whom their souls rely on,
   Makes them kings and priests to God.
'Tis His love His people raises
   Over self to reign as kings,
And as priests, His solemn praises
   Each for a thank-off'ring brings.

Saviour, if of Zion's city
   I through grace a member am,
Let the world deride or pity,
   I will glory in Thy name :
Fading is the worldling's pleasure,
   All his boasted pomp and show :
Solid joys and lasting treasure,
   None but Zion's children know.

"Olney Hymns" was published in 1779. In that year Newton became rector of a church in London, and died there December 31, 1807. Thus he had a long life after his conversion. It was a very useful life. Wesley and Whitefield were his friends. Among his converts were Claudius Buchanan, the great missionary to the East Indies, and Thomas Scott, the eminent Bible commentator. He preached almost to the time of his death, asking, "Shall the old African blasphemer stop while he can speak?" And he still preaches through his strong and spirited hymns.

" God Moves in a Mysterious Way "
William Cowper

ONE of the saddest lives ever lived was that of the author of our hymn, William Cowper. He was born at Great Berkhampstead, England, in 1731. His father was rector of the church there. His mother died when he was six years old, and that was his first great sorrow.

His second misfortune was when, at the age of ten, he was sent to Westminster School. He was a delicate, sensitive lad, and the other boys tormented him till he was almost crazy.

After this time, when he was studying law, he fell in love with his cousin ; but her father would not let him marry her. That was his third great grief.

He was not a success as a lawyer. A friend obtained for him a position as clerk in the House of Lords ; but when the shrinking young man learned that he would need to be examined before the bar of the House of Lords, he became so terrified at the prospect that he tried to commit suicide.

Ever since the age of twenty, Cowper's mind had been giving way. He was put into an insane asylum, where a sympathetic doctor did much for him ; but all his life after that was clouded with his fearful disease. Indeed, there were only three bright spots in it.

One of these was his friendship with the Unwins, and especially with Mrs. Unwin, who nursed him tenderly.   Another was his friendship with Rev. John Newton, a strong character with a history very different from Cowper's and yet with tastes much like his.   The third was his poetry, which became a great solace to him, as it has remained a great blessing to the world.

Cowper wrote a number of great secular poems. The rollicking narrative, "John Gilpin," is well known.   His greatest work is a long poem in blank verse, "The Task," one of the wisest books ever written, and one of the most charming.   But we have to do just now with his religious verses.

It was John Newton who proposed, perhaps to divert his friend's mind from his melancholy, that they two should write a volume of hymns.   The result was the famous "Olney Hymns," named from the town in which the two were living.   These hymns were composed from 1767 to 1779.   There are 349 of these hymns, and Cowper is said to have written 66 of them.

Selections from the Olney Hymns are to be found in all hymn-books.   Among those by Cowper are, "O for a closer walk with God," "Sometimes a light surprises," "Hark, my soul, it is the Lord," "Jesus, where'er Thy people meet," "What various hindrances we meet," and the greatest of his hymns, "There is a fountain filled with blood."

Then, there is the magnificent hymn, "God moves in a mysterious way."   It is said that Cowper wrote this hymn after recovering from one of his fits of madness, in the course of which he had tried to drown himself in the River Ouse, but had been providentially prevented. The hymn was written about the year 1773. The tender, loving poet lingered on for many years, and his sad life did not come to an end till 1800.

Here is our hymn :—

> God moves in a mysterious way
>   His wonders to perform ;
> He plants His footsteps in the sea,
>   And rides upon the storm.
>
> Ye fearful saints, fresh courage take !
>   The clouds ye so much dread
> Are big with mercy, and will break
>   In blessings on your head.
>
> Judge not the Lord by feeble sense,
>   But trust Him for His grace :
> Behind a frowning providence
>   He hides a smiling face.
>
> His purposes will ripen fast,
>   Unfolding every hour ;
> The bud may have a bitter taste,
>   But sweet will be the flower.
>
> Blind unbelief is sure to err,
>   And scan his work in vain ;
> God is His own interpreter,
>   And He will make it plain.

" Shepherd of Tender Youth "
Clement of Alexandria

THIS hymn is one of great interest, because, outside the New Testament hymns, it is the oldest Christian hymn whose authorship is known. Of course it was not written in English, but in Greek. The author lived seventeen centuries ago. His name was Clement, and he is called Clement of Alexandria, to distinguish him from other men of the same name, and because he was head of the great Christian school in that Egyptian city. He had been a heathen philosopher, and he did not become a Christian until he had studied the new religion under at least six different teachers, so that when he did take up Christianity, he went into it with a full understanding, and became a powerful teacher of it.

Among the books that Clement wrote is one called "The Instructor," explaining in a very enthusiastic way the teachings of Christ. At the close of this book is our hymn. No one knows just when it was written, but Clement was driven away from Alexandria by persecution in A. D. 202, and died about A. D. 220, so that the hymn is just about one thousand seven hundred years old.

The translation into English, strange to say, is very recent, for the work was not done till 1846. In

that year Rev. Henry Martyn Dexter, a Congregational minister of Manchester, N. H., translated the
old Greek poem to use with a sermon on Deut. 32 : 7,
"Remember the days of old." First he put the
Greek into prose, and then he put his prose translation, or as much of it as he thought suitable, into
poetry. The result is that it is not a very accurate
translation, though a very spirited one. The hymn
was first printed in *The Congregationalist*, the paper
of which Dr. Dexter afterward became the editor,
in the number for December 21, 1849. And here
it is :—

> Shepherd of tender youth,
> Guiding in love and truth
>   Through devious ways :
> Christ, our triumphant King,
> We come Thy name to sing,
> And here our children bring,
>   To shout Thy praise.
>
> Thou art our holy Lord,
> O all-subduing Word,
>   Healer of strife :
> Thou didst Thyself abase,
> That from sin's deep disgrace
> Thou mightest save our race,
>   And give us life.
>
> Thou art the great High Priest,
> Thou hast prepared the feast
>   Of heavenly love :
> While in our mortal pain,
> None calls on Thee in vain :
> Help Thou dost not disdain,
>   Help from above.

Ever be Thou our Guide,
Our Shepherd and our Pride,
  Our Staff and Song :
Jesus, Thou Christ of God,
By Thy perennial word
Lead us where Thou hast trod ;
  Make our faith strong.

So now, and till we die,
Sound we Thy praises high,
  And joyful sing :
Infants, and the glad throng
Who to Thy Church belong
Unite to swell the song
To Christ our King.

" Jesus, Still Lead On "
Count Zinzendorf

THE noble Nicolaus Ludwig, Count von Zinzendorf, was born in Dresden, Germany, May 26,
1700. While he was a school boy he heard of the
missionary work in the East Indies, and formed a
missionary society among his boy friends, called
" The Order of the Grain of Mustard Seed." When
he was fifteen years old, he entered into a covenant
with a friend of his, promising that he would give
his life to the spread of Christianity, especially in the
places where no one else wanted to go.

One day he saw the famous picture, Sternberg's
" Ecce Homo," " Behold the Man," showing Pilate
presenting Christ to the mocking throng. Beneath
it is a Latin motto which, translated, is :—

> " I have done this for thee;
> What hast thou done for Me ? "

The picture and motto made a deep impression upon
him, and caused him to renew his vows of whole-
hearted service. When he was married, in 1722, he
and his noble wife agreed, on their wedding day, to
lay aside their rank, and give themselves up to the
winning of men to Christ.

The great opportunity of Zinzendorf's life came to

him when a band of persecuted Moravians, led by
Christian David, settled in his own town of Berthelsdorf. They had been driven from home by the
Roman Catholics, and their condition moved Zinzendorf to give them aid. He soon became deeply
attached to the heroic Protestants, and became their
second leader. He established them in their famous
community of Herrnhut, made laws for them, fash-
ioned for them a beautiful order of service, and gave
his life to the development of their church.

How Zinzendorf and his Moravians founded Moravian missions is one of the most thrilling stories in
all missionary annals. They heard of the great need
for the gospel in Greenland and among the slaves of
the West Indies, and at once, with eagerness, they
sprang to meet the need. The sufferings of those
pioneer missionaries are almost beyond belief.
Poverty, disease, imprisonment, hostility, loneliness,
failure, all kinds of trials, were met by them with
patience and undaunted zeal. We call William
Carey the founder of modern missions; but when
he went to India, the Moravians already had 165
missionaries at work in all parts of the world.

In all this labor Zinzendorf was a leader. He had
many enemies, and at last the constant misrepre-
sentations of these foes procured his banishment from
his native land. It was during this exile that he
visited America. He preached Christ zealously
among the Indians, and at Bethlehem, Penn., he
established what is to this day the great centre of
Moravian work on this continent.

In 1749 Zinzendorf was entirely cleared of the

charges that had been made against him, and the government not only asked him to return, but requested him to form other model communities like Herrnhut. So the great and good man passed the last years of his life peacefully at Berthelsdorf, and when he died in 1760, his body was carried to the grave by thirty-two missionaries and preachers, from Holland, England, Ireland, North America, and Greenland.

The Moravians made much of song, as they still do. Zinzendorf wrote more that two thousand hymns, all of them expressing his deep devotion. One of the best-known of these was translated by John Wesley, and begins, "Jesus, Thy blood and righteousness." But of all Zinzendorf's writings, the favorite is certainly the hymn here given, " Jesus, still lead on." It seems to embody all of Count Zinzendorf's heroic life. I give the translation made by Miss Jane Borthwick :—

Jesus, still lead on,
Till our rest be won ;
And although the way be cheerless,
We will follow, calm and fearless ;
Guide us by Thy hand
To our Fatherland.

If the way be drear,
If the foe be near,
Let not faithless fears o'ertake us,
Let not faith and hope forsake us ;
For, through many a foe,
To our home we go.

When we seek relief
From a long-felt grief,
When temptations come, alluring,
Make us patient and enduring ;
Show us that bright shore
Where we weep no more.

Jesus, still lead on,
Till our rest be won ;
Heavenly Leader, still direct us,
Still support, console, protect us,
Till we safely stand
In our Fatherland.

"O Master, Let Me Walk with Thee"
Washington Gladden

REV. WASHINGTON GLADDEN, D. D., LL. D., who wrote this beautiful hymn which is in most of our hymn-books, is a distinguished Congregational clergyman. He was born in Pottsgrove, Penn., February 11, 1836. He was until recently active in the ministry, being a busy pastor in Columbus, O., and he has been honored with the chief post in his denomination, the moderatorship of the National Council.

Dr. Gladden has been an editor of *The Independent*, and also of *Sunday Afternoon*. It was while he was editor of the latter magazine that he wrote the poem from which his famous hymn was taken. It appeared in March, 1879, with three eight-line stanzas. The second of these, which is not included in the hymn as printed in our hymn-books, was as follows : —

O Master, let me walk with Thee
Before the taunting Pharisee ;
Help me to bear the sting of spite,
The hate of men who hide Thy light,
The sore distrust of souls sincere
Who cannot read Thy judgments clear,
The dullness of the multitude,
Who dimly guess that Thou are good.

These lines Dr. Gladden himself would exclude from the hymn, for he says he had no intention of writing a hymn when the poem was composed ; and yet they are remarkably fine.   The remainder of the poem, as we sing it, is this : —

> O Master, let me walk with Thee
> In lowly paths of service free ;
> Tell me Thy secret ; help me bear
> The strain of toil, the fret of care.
>
> Help me the slow of heart to move
> By some clear winning word of love ;
> Teach me the wayward feet to stay,
> And guide them in the homeward way.
>
> Teach me Thy patience ; still with Thee
> In closer, dearer company,
> In work that keeps faith sweet and strong,
> In trust that triumphs over wrong.
>
> In hope that sends a shining ray
> Far down the future's broadening way,
> In peace that only Thou canst give,
> With Thee, O Master, let me live !

Dr. Gladden has written other hymns, though none have won so great favor as this.   He has written many books of essays, studies of social questions, volumes on the Bible, and one charming collection of Christmas stories.   He is a favorite public speaker and lecturer.

"I Do Not Ask, O Lord, That Life May Be "

Adelaide Anne Procter

ADELAIDE ANNE PROCTER was the daughter of the famous poet, Bryan Waller Procter, who wrote under the name of " Barry Cornwall." She was born in London in 1825, and died in London in 1864, in her thirty-ninth year.

She was a precocious child. Before she could write herself she got her mother to copy for her into an album some of her favorite poems. " It looks," wrote her friend, Charles Dickens, "as if she had carried the book about as another little girl might have carried a doll." She became a fine scholar, easily learning mathematics, French, Italian, and German. She was skilful in playing on the piano and in drawing. She was a great reader.

Her father had no idea that his girl could write poetry till he saw her first little poem in print. Dickens published many of her poems in his magazine without knowing who wrote them, because she sent them under the pen name of Mary Berwick. This was because Dickens and her father were warm friends, and she was afraid that if she offered her verses under her own name the great novelist would take them to please her father, even though they might be unworthy, or that he would be placed in an awkward predicament if he wanted to return them. "Perhaps," Dickens wrote afterward, "it requires an editor's experience of the profoundly unreasonable grounds on which he is often urged to accept unsuitable articles—such as having been to school with the writer's husband's brother-in-law, or having lent an alpen-stock in Switzerland to the writer's wife's nephew, when that interesting stranger had broken his own—fully to appreciate the delicacy and self-respect of this resolution."

In 1858 Miss Procter published a volume of poems, "Legends and Lyrics," which at once placed her very close to Mrs. Browning and Miss Rossetti as a poet. From this volume her hymns are taken. Besides the one printed here we often use "I thank Thee, O my God, who made The earth so bright," "The shadows of the evening hours," "One by one the sands are flowing," and "Strive, yet I do not promise." She wrote the famous song, "The Lost Chord," which Sir Arthur S. Sullivan set to music while sitting by the death-bed of his brother.

In 1851 Miss Procter became a Roman Catholic, and gave herself up to the care of the poor in such an eager way that she lost her health and brought on a sickness which confined her to her bed for fifteen months, finally carrying her off. Always cheerful and vivacious, during this long confinement to the sick-room her cheerfulness, says Dickens, never left her, and the novelist tells how she passed from earth with the exclamation, "It has come at last!" and with a bright, happy smile.

The hymn before us was first written in a form

different from that which it finally assumed, and was entitled "Resignation." In later editions of her poems it was changed to its present form and was given the title, "*Per Pacem ad Lucem*," that is, "Through Peace to Light." Here is the hymn in full.

> I do not ask, O Lord, that life may be
>   A pleasant road ;
> I do not ask that Thou wouldst take from me
>   Aught of its load;
>
> I do not ask that flowers should always spring
>   Beneath my feet ;
> I know too well the poison and the sting
>   Of things too sweet.
>
> For one thing only, Lord, dear Lord, I plead ;
>   Lead me aright —
> Though strength should falter, and though
>   heart should bleed —
>   Through peace to light.
>
> I do not ask, O Lord, that Thou shouldst shed
>   Full radiance here ;
> Give but a ray of peace, that I may tread
>   Without a fear.
>
> I do not ask my cross to understand,
>   My way to see ;
> Better in darkness just to feel Thy hand,
>   And follow Thee.
>
> Joy is like restless day ; but peace divine
>   Like quiet night ;
> Lead me, O Lord, till perfect day shall shine,
>   Through peace to light.

"Walk in the Light: So Shalt Thou Know"
Bernard Barton

BERNARD BARTON, who wrote this hymn, was often called, like Whittier, "The Quaker Poet." He was born in a Quaker family in London, January 31, 1784, and he was a Quaker all his life.

Educated in a Quaker school, he worked in a shop for eight years, then became a coal and corn dealer, then a private tutor, and finally spent the last forty years of his life as a bank clerk. He died February 19, 1849.

Barton wrote ten volumes of poems. His first volume, issued in 1812, won the favorable notice of Robert Southey. The poems he published in 1820 obtained for him the friendship of a very different man, Lord Byron. Sir Robert Peel gained for him a state pension of $500, which he received for several years.

About twenty of Barton's hymns have found their way into use, one of the best known being "Lamp of our feet, whereby we trace Our path when wont to stray." The hymn before us, however, is by far his best-known hymn. Published in 1826, it has been found in many of our leading hymn-books. The theme is one that is very dear to all members of the society of Friends, who lay so much stress upon "the inner light."

I give the hymn with all its six stanzas, though some hymn-books omit the fourth, and nearly all omit the second : —

Walk in the light : so shalt thou know
That fellowship of love
His spirit only can bestow,
Who reigns in light above.

Walk in the light : and sin abhorred
Shall ne'er defile again ;
The blood of Jesus Christ thy Lord
Shall cleanse from every stain.

Walk in the light : and thou shalt find
Thy heart made truly His
Who dwells in cloudless light enshrined,
In whom no darkness is.

Walk in the light : and thou shalt own
Thy darkness passed away,
Because that Light hath on thee shone
In which is perfect day.

Walk in the light : and e'en the tomb
No fearful shade shall wear ;
Glory shall chase away its gloom,
For Christ hath conquered there.

Walk in the light : and thine shall be
A path, though thorny, bright ;
For God, by grace, shall dwell in thee,
And God Himself is light.

"America, the Beautiful."

Katharine Lee Bates.

THE United States has a number of national hymns, each with many fine qualities, and each also with some defects that prevent its acceptance as the final and entirely satisfactory national hymn. A new hymn, entitled "America, the Beautiful," seems to me to be finer and more appropriate than any of the others, and I should not be surprised to see it growing in favor till it has become the recognized hymn of our country.

This hymn was written by Miss Katharine Lee Bates, who was born in Falmouth, Mass., in 1859. She was graduated from Wellesley College in 1880, and then taught mathematics, classics, and English in the Natick, Mass., high school, and later taught Latin in Dana Hall, Wellesley. In 1885 she began her work as teacher of English literature in the famous college for girls, and since 1891 has been the professor of that important subject. Certainly no one could fill her place more excellently, and no one is a greater favorite with the scholars.

Travel has added to Miss Bates's splendid equipment, for she has spent a year in England, mainly at Oxford, a year in France and Spain, and a third year in Switzerland, Egypt, Syria, and Italy, not to speak of several summers spent in travel or study abroad. These extensive travels are mentioned jovially in the following amusing "biography" of Professor Bates that appeared in a college paper, *The Echo :* —

" Professor Katharine Lee Bates was born midway between ex-President Roosevelt and William J. Bryan, at Falmouth, Mass., where her cradle may be seen on exhibition in the town hall.

"She entered Wellesley College one hundred years after the signing of the Declaration of Independence, and graduated as president of her class in 1880.

" Since then Miss Bates has followed the profession of a teacher whenever she couldn't help it, and has written many books.

"She has wandered from the Charles River to the Jordan, and from Pegan Hill to the Pyramids, recently becoming a detective in the 'Sure as Nails' Detective Agency. She now lives in the 'Scarab' on Curve Street in our town."

Miss Bates has written many books and edited many more. The books she has edited are nearly all editions of English classics. Her "very own" books are volumes of poems, stories, travels, and books on English and American literature.

Miss Bates's patriotic hymn, "America, the Beautiful," was written in Colorado in the summer of 1893, after a visit to "the White City." It was left in the author's note-book for the next two years, and was not printed till July, 1895. Then it came out in *The Congregationalist.* The present form of the hymn, however, differs quite materially from that first version.

The original version of the hymn was set to music

by Silas G. Pratt, and printed in Part II. of "Famous Songs," published in 1895 by Bryan, Taylor, and Company of New York. Several other composers have written music for the lovely words, and among these various settings my own preference is for the very rich and noble music composed by Mr. Charles S. Brown. Mr. Brown's composition is to be found in the Christian Endeavor hymn-books, "Junior Carols," "The Praise Book," and "Jubilant Praise."

Here are the words of the hymn, and the version given has passed under Miss Bates's eyes and has been declared to be the correct one : —

O beautiful for spacious skies,
　For amber waves of grain,
For purple mountain majesties
　Above the fruited plain !
　　America !　America !
　God shed His grace on thee
And crown thy good with brotherhood
　From sea to shining sea !

O beautiful for pilgrim feet,
　Whose stern, impassioned stress
A thoroughfare for freedom beat
　Across the wilderness !
　　America !　America !
　God mend thine every flaw,
Confirm thy soul in self-control,
　Thy liberty in law !

O beautiful for heroes proved
　In liberating strife,
Who more than self their country loved,
　And mercy more than life !

America !   America !
May God thy gold refine,
Till all success be nobleness,
And every gain divine !

O beautiful for patriot dream
That sees beyond the years
Thine alabaster cities gleam
Undimmed by human tears !
America !   America !
God shed His grace on thee
And crown thy good with brotherhood
From sea to shining sea !

"Saviour! Teach Me Day by Day"

Jane Elizabeth Leeson

ABOUT the author of this hymn, Miss Jane Elizabeth Leeson, very little is known. This is because of her extreme modesty and retiring disposition. She wrote a dozen volumes, but insisted that all of them should first be published without her name. She was born in England in 1815, and died in 1883. For many years she was a member of the Church of England, but toward the end of her life she became a Roman Catholic.

Nearly all of Miss Leeson's books were poetical, and nearly all were written for children. Perhaps the best known is " Hymns and Scenes of Childhood." The hymn here given, taken from that book, is by far the most famous of her hymns, but another that is often sung is " Sweet the lessons Jesus taught."

Saviour ! teach me, day by day,
Love's sweet lesson to obey ;
Sweeter lesson cannot be,
Loving Him who first loved me.

With a childlike heart of love,
At Thy bidding may I move ;
Prompt to serve and follow Thee,
Loving Him who first loved me.

Teach me all Thy steps to trace,
Strong to follow in Thy grace;
Learning how to love from Thee,
Loving Him who first loved me.

Love in loving finds employ —
In obedience all her joy;
Ever new that joy will be,
Loving Him who first loved me.

Thus may I rejoice to show
That I feel the love I owe;
Singing, till Thy face I see,
Of His love who first loved me.

"Come, Thou Fount of Every Blessing."

Robert Robinson.

THIS hymn, which is one of the noblest ever written, was composed by Rev. Robert Robinson. Its writer was born in Swaffham, England, September 27, 1735, and died as he had wished to die, "softly, suddenly, and alone," being found dead in his bed on the morning of June 9, 1790.

He was a poor boy, the only support of his mother, "and she was a widow." At the age of fourteen, he became apprentice to a barber in London, where he seems to have been none of the steadiest. At one time he made a gypsy fortune-teller drunk, and while she was under the influence of liquor she prophesied that the lad would "see his children and his grandchildren."

The prophecy made a deep impression upon the young fellow, and he decided to make something of himself, for the sake of these unborn descendants. He became a convert of the great preacher, George Whitefield, and at once began to preach on his own account. He joined the Baptists, and was made pastor of a small church in Cambridge.

In that university town he passed nearly all of the remainder of his life, honored even by the scholars of the place, since he was himself also a scholar by the power of his mind, though he had none of a scholar's training. He published several volumes,

321

and his sermons are full of a quaint common sense. The great preacher, Robert Hall, who followed him in the same church, was his spiritual successor also, just as, in later years, the eminent Spurgeon became the disciple of Robert Hall.

Robinson was a practical man, and did not hesitate to take up farming to eke out his scanty income. He was a man of large and liberal temper, though a true believer in orthodox religion. For this reason I am inclined to doubt the anecdote of Mr. Robinson's conversation with a lady whom he is said to have met in a stage coach. She forced the talk to the subject of religion, and at last quoted his own hymn, " Come, thou Fount of every blessing," speaking of the blessings it had brought to her. Upon this Robinson is said to have exclaimed, " Madam, I am the poor unhappy man who composed that hymn, many years ago, and I would give a thousand worlds, if I had them, to enjoy the feelings I had then."

Mr. Robinson is not known to have written more than two hymns. One of these begins, " Mighty God, while angels bless Thee," and the other is the following hymn, which was composed probably in 1757.

> Come, thou Fount of every blessing,
>   Tune my heart to sing Thy grace ;
> Streams of mercy, never ceasing,
>   Call for songs of loudest praise.
>
> Teach me some melodious sonnet,
>   Sung by flaming tongues above ;
> Praise the mount !   I'm fixed upon it,
>   Mount of God's unchanging love !

Here I raise my Ebenezer;
  Hither by Thy help I'm come;
And I hope, by Thy good pleasure,
  Safely to arrive at home.

Jesus sought me when a stranger,
  Wandering from the fold of God;
He, to rescue me from danger,
  Interposed His precious blood.

Oh, to grace how great a debtor
  Daily I'm constrained to be!
Let that grace now, like a fetter,
  Bind my wandering heart to Thee.

Prone to wander, Lord, I feel it;
  Prone to leave the God I love;
Here's my heart; oh, take and seal it,—
  Seal it for Thy courts above!

" Sunset and Evening Star "
Alfred Tennyson

ALFRED TENNYSON, the greatest poet of Victoria's reign, left to the world no legacy more precious than the hymn before us.

He was born on August 6, 1809, and with his brother Charles he published a volume of poems in his eighteenth year. At Trinity College, Cambridge, he won a prize for a poem, and when he was twenty-one he put forth a book of poems which at once made him famous. He succeeded Wordsworth as poet laureate, and for more than sixty years was the chief man of letters of the Anglo-Saxon race. In 1883 he became Lord Tennyson, and on October 6, 1892, the great poet passed away.

In 1889, when Tennyson was in his eighty-first year, he wrote the hymn, "Crossing the Bar." It is the only hymn he ever wrote, if we except the little children's hymn, "O man, forgive thy mortal foe," in "The Promise of May," and the opening stanzas of "In Memoriam," "Strong Son of God, immortal Love," which are sometimes used as a hymn. The poem was written after a walk along the shore with the sound of the sea in his ears, and soon after his return he showed the verses to his son, who said at once, "That is the crown of your life's work." "It came in a moment," said Tennyson.

Some lines of the hymn have been misunderstood. By the Pilot, the poet meant, as he said, "that Divine and Unseen who is always guiding us." "The dark" means, he said, "the Valley of the Shadow of Death." The "call for me" is the voice of the turning tide, ready to float the vessel of life out into the great unknown. The pilot, of course, is in charge of a ship while it is crossing the bar; but in our voyage of life we do not see our Pilot "face to face" until after we have crossed the bar. Tennyson was profoundly religious, and this poem beautifully expresses the deepest thoughts of his heart. Once he said, "What the sun is to that flower, that Jesus Christ is to my soul."

"Crossing the Bar" is placed, at Tennyson's request, at the end of all editions of his poems. It was most fitting that it should have been sung during the poet's funeral in Westminster Abbey. Lady Tennyson herself wrote music for it, and another setting has been made by Sir Joseph Barnby. The words of the hymn are printed here just as Tennyson wrote them :—

   Sunset and evening star,
      And one clear call for me !
   And may there be no moaning of the bar
      When I put out to sea.

   But such a tide as moving seems asleep,
      Too full for sound and foam,
   When that which drew from out the boundless deep
      Turns again home.

Twilight and evening bell,
And after that the dark !
And may there be no sadness of farewell
When I embark ;

For, though from out our bourne of time and place
The flood may bear me far,
I hope to see my Pilot face to face
When I have crost the bar.

" Immortal Love, for Ever Full "
John Greenleaf Whittier

THE beloved Quaker poet, John Greenleaf Whittier, was born at Haverhill, Mass., December 17, 1807. He died September 7, 1892. At first he was a farmer's boy and a shoemaker. Then he edited a number of papers, among them *The Pennsylvania Freeman*, published in Philadelphia. Because of his antislavery principles, the office of this paper was burned by a mob.

Whittier became one of the great antislavery leaders of the country, and many of his poems are bugle-blasts for that cause. The poet was at one time a member of the Massachusetts legislature. He wrote the stirring hymn for the opening of the Centennial Exposition in Philadelphia. His most famous poem is probably "Snow-Bound."

Many hymns have been taken from Whittier's works, usually from the midst of longer poems. He himself wrote modestly: "I am really not a hymn-writer, for the good reason that I know nothing of music. Only a very few of my pieces were written for singing. A good hymn is the best use to which poetry can be devoted, but I do not claim that I have succeeded in composing one."

Notwithstanding, there are few hymns in our hymn-books that we would not rather lose than the beautiful religious poem given below. The seven stanzas usually sung are taken from a very much longer poem, one of Whittier's best, " Our Master," published in 1856. It is often made to begin with different stanzas ; I give all that are ever used as a hymn.

Among other hymns by Whittier are " All as God wills, who wisely heeds," " Dear Lord and Father of mankind," " O sometimes gleams upon our sight," and " When on my day of life the night is falling."

>Immortal love, for ever full,
>　For ever flowing free,
>For ever shared, for ever whole,
>　A never ebbing sea !

>Our outward lips confess the name
>　All other names above ;
>Love only knoweth whence it came,
>　And comprehendeth love.

>We may not climb the heavenly steeps
>　To bring the Lord Christ down ;
>In vain we search the lowest deeps,
>　For Him no depths can drown.

>But warm, sweet, tender, even yet
>　A present help is He ;
>And Faith has still its Olivet,
>　And love its Galilee.

>The healing of His seamless dress
>　Is by our beds of pain ;
>We touch Him in life's throng and press,
>　And we are whole again.

Through Him the first fond prayers are said
  Our lips of childhood frame,
The last low whispers of our dead
  Are burdened with His name.

O Lord and Master of us all !
  Whate'er our name or sign,
We own Thy sway, we hear Thy call,
  We test our lives by Thine.

"Shall We Gather at the River?"

Robert Lowry

THIS beautiful and very popular hymn was written by Rev. Robert Lowry, D. D. He was born in Philadelphia, March 12, 1826, and died at a good old age in 1899. Educated at Lewisburg University in Pennsylvania, he became a Baptist minister in New York, Brooklyn, and other cities, and professor of *belles-lettres* in Lewisburg University.

Dr. Lowry was editor of ten or a dozen of the most popular Sunday-school song-books ever published, and he contributed to these some of their best hymns and tunes. Among his hymns that are most widely sung are "My life flows on in endless song," "One more day's work for Jesus," and "Where is my wandering boy to-night?" For all of these he also wrote the tunes.

But Dr. Lowry's most famous hymn is "Shall we gather at the river?" He wrote the words when a pastor in Brooklyn, on a hot July day in 1864. A very severe epidemic was raging in Brooklyn, and hundreds were passing over the river of death. Dr. Lowry was thinking of the sad scenes all around him when the question arose in his mind, "Shall we meet again? We are parting at the river of death; shall we meet at the river of life?"

With his heart full of these thoughts, he seated himself at his parlor organ, and both the words and the music of the famous hymn came to him as if by inspiration. It was published the following year in "Happy Voices," as a hymn of five stanzas and a chorus :—

Shall we gather at the river,
   Where bright angel-feet have trod,
With its crystal tide forever
   Flowing by the throne of God?

Chorus :
Yes, we'll gather at the river,
   The beautiful, the beautiful river;
Gather with the saints at the river
   That flows by the throne of God.

On the margin of the river,
   Washing up its silver spray,
We will walk and worship ever
   All the happy, golden day.

Ere we reach the shining river,
   Lay we every burden down;
Grace our spirits will deliver,
   And provide a robe and crown.

At the smiling of the river,
   Mirror of the Saviour's face,
Saints, whom death will never sever,
   Lift their songs of saving grace.

Soon we'll reach the silver river;
   Soon our pilgrimage will cease;
Soon our happy hearts will quiver
   With the melody of peace.

"Throw Out the Life-Line"
Edward Smith Ufford

DR. CUYLER, when he heard Mr. Sankey sing the stirring song, "Throw Out the Life-Line," remarked, "There is more electricity in that song than in any other I have heard." It is indeed a rousing appeal, and it has done and is doing a mighty work in moving the consciences of men.

The writer of the song, Rev. Edward Smith Ufford, is still alive, traveling widely and giving illustrated religious lectures based upon his great hymn. He uses his fine collection of life-saving apparatus as a series of object-lessons, pressing home spiritual truths in a very forceful way. He is a man of noble Christian character, and personal contact with his strong faith and burning zeal has been a tonic for many thousands.

Mr. Ufford was born in Newark, N. J., in 1851. He was educated at Stratford Academy in Connecticut, and at Bates Theological Seminary, Maine. He has held several pastorates in Baptist churches, and has edited several song-books.

"Throw Out the Life-Line" was prompted by a drill which Mr. Ufford witnessed at the life-saving station on Point Allerton, near Boston. A ship had been wrecked near the place, and the memory of that, together with the sight of the life-line flung out

far over the water and the energetic action of the
life-saving crew, put the thought of the song into
Mr. Ufford's mind.

When he reached home he wrote the song rapidly,
and then sat down to his organ (for he is a musician
as well as poet), and in fifteen minutes he had composed the world-famous melody. In 1888 the song
was published in sheet-music form, and in 1890, har-
monized by Mr. Stebbins, it was published in a
song-book. Here are the thrilling words : —

> Throw out the life-line across the dark wave;
> There is a brother whom some one should save;
> Somebody's brother: oh, who then will dare
> To throw out the life-line, his peril to share?
>
> Throw out the life-line with hand quick and strong:
> Why do you tarry, why linger so long?
> See! he is sinking; oh, hasten to-day
> And out with the life-boat! away, then, away!
>
> Throw out the life-line to danger-fraught men
> Sinking in anguish where you've never been;
> Winds of temptation and billows of woe
> Will soon hurl them out where the dark waters flow.
>
> Soon will the season of rescue be o'er;
> Soon will they drift to eternity's shore;
> Haste, then, my brother, no time for delay,
> But throw out the life-line and save them to-day.

Mr. Ufford tells many stories of the results that
have come from the singing of this hymn. Once in
Pennsylvania a set of men were playing cards and

drinking in a club-room. Another room in the
same building had been rented for religious meetings, and suddenly the words of "Throw Out the
Life-Line," sung sweetly by a young woman, with a
strong chorus taking up the refrain, broke in upon
their merriment. The revelry was hushed. At last
one player threw down his cards. "If what they
are singing is right," he said, "then we are wrong."
He went home, and before long the others followed
his manly example. The club was broken up by
that one song. In countless other instances the
hymn has been used to arouse men to a sense of
their sin.

But of course its chief use has been to prompt
Christians to take up evangelistic work. In this it
has been exceedingly successful. Thousands of
Christians have been moved by its tender pleading
to leave their selfish endeavors, go down to the tem-
pest-torn beach, and do their best to rescue those
that are battling with the waves of sin. How many
"Life-Line Leagues" and similar organizations
have been named from the hymn no one knows.
It has done a glorious work.

"Souls of Men, Why Will Ye Scatter?"

Frederick William Faber

THE author of this hymn was a Roman Catholic, and yet many of his beautiful hymns are sung with great pleasure by Protestants. Frederick William Faber was born in England, June 28, 1814. He was a studious boy, and was sent to Oxford University. There he came under the influence of John Henry Newman, who wrote "Lead, Kindly Light." The two men were very much alike in their spirits, and when Newman became a Roman Catholic it might have been foreseen that Faber would follow.

This, however, did not happen at once. Faber traveled for four years through Europe, and then became a rector of the Church of England. He was a successful preacher and a greatly beloved pastor, but at last he decided to go over to the Roman Catholic Church. First at Birmingham, and then in London, he served as a priest, and died on September 26, 1863, at the early age of 49.

Dr. Faber wrote much in both prose and verse. His hymns number in all 150. They are marked by great sweetness and by many literary excellencies, and some of them have attained to wide popularity. Among the most famous are the following : "There's a wideness in God's mercy," "Hark ! hark ! my soul, angelic songs are swelling," "O Paradise, O Paradise!" "Sweet Saviour, bless us ere we go," "O God! Thy power is wonderful," "O gift of gifts! O grace of faith!" "God's glory is a wondrous thing," "My God! How wonderful Thou art," "I worship Thee, sweet will of God."

Faber's most famous hymn is the one printed below. It is usually referred to as "There's a wideness in God's mercy," from its most frequently used stanza; but the first stanza begins, "Souls of men, why will ye scatter?" It was published in Faber's "Oratory Hymns" in 1854, and the full form is as follows: —

> Souls of men, why will ye scatter
>   Like a crowd of frightened sheep?
> Foolish hearts, why will ye wander
>   From a love so true and deep?
> Was there ever kindest shepherd
>   Half so gentle, half so sweet,
> As the Saviour who would have us
>   Come and gather at His feet?
>
> It is God: His love looks mighty,
>   But is mightier than it seems.
> 'Tis our Father, and His fondness
>   Goes far out beyond our dreams.
> There's a wideness in God's mercy,
>   Like the wideness of the sea;
> There's a kindness in His justice,
>   Which is more than liberty.
>
> For the love of God is broader
>   Than the measures of man's mind,
> And the heart of the Eternal
>   Is most wonderfully kind.

But we make His love too narrow
  By false limits of our own,
And we magnify His strictness
  With a zeal He will not own.

There is plentiful redemption
  In the blood that has been shed ;
There is joy for all the members
  In the sorrows of the Head.
If our love were but more simple,
  We should take Him at His word ;
And our lives would be all sunshine
  In the sweetness of our Lord.

"Hail to the Brightness of Zion's Glad Morning"

Thomas Hastings

THIS beautiful hymn was written by Thomas Hastings, one of the greatest of American hymn-writers. He was born at Washington, Litchfield County, Conn., October 15, 1784—a century and a quarter ago. His father was a physician, and in 1796 he removed with his family to Clinton, N. Y. They had to make their way through what was then an unbroken wilderness, and they went in sleighs and ox-sleds.

Young Hastings was made familiar with all the duties of a farm boy. The winter gave him his only time for schooling, and he was glad to walk to school six miles every day. A twelve-cent primer of music consisting of only four small pages gave him his first knowledge of that difficult art. He became a leader of the village choir, and entered upon the study of music in earnest. After many attempts, he at last got a situation as a music-teacher—in Bridgewater and Brookfield, N. Y. The young people of those singing-schools were bent on having a good time, but Mr. Hastings made them attend also to the business in hand, and produced splendid results. In 1816, Mr. Hastings compiled a famous music-book, "Musica Sacra." He made it a business to train church choirs and teach congregations how to sing, and did this in a number of New York cities. In 1822 he published a book, "The Musical Taste," arguing that religion has a right to music as one of its instruments as well as to speech.

In 1823, Mr. Hastings became editor of the *Recorder*, published in Utica. He was to get $600 a year if the paper prospered, but only $300 if it did not! He remained with the paper till, in 1832, twelve churches in New York combined to obtain his services as a trainer of their choirs, and from that time till his death, in 1872, Dr. Hastings (for the college degree of doctor of music was given to him) lived in New York, and became one of the most powerful of American forces for the development of religious music.

In spite of a distressing eye-trouble which hindered him all his life (he was, with other troubles, exceedingly near-sighted) he accomplished a wonderful amount of work. He is said to have composed more than one thousand hymn tunes, the most famous being Toplady, the tune of "Rock of Ages," and Ortonville, the tune of "Majestic sweetness sits enthroned." He is said to have written six hundred hymns, though most of them were not signed. He published fifty volumes of church music. Probably Fanny Crosby alone has written a larger number of hymns that are in common use—American writers alone being considered, and the Wesleys left out of account. Among Dr. Hastings's famous hymns are: "Child of sin and sorrow," "Delay not, delay not, O sinner, draw near," "Gently, Lord, O gently lead us," " How calm and beautiful the morn," " Now be the gospel banner," " O tell me, thou life and delight of my soul," " To-day the Saviour calls," and " He that goeth forth with weeping."

Dr. Hastings was a Presbyterian, and a man of great nobility of character. His famous son, President Hastings of the Union Theological Seminary, said of him, " He was a devout and earnest Christian, a hard student, and a resolute worker, not laying aside his pen until three days before his death."

Probably Dr. Hastings's greatest hymn is the one given below, which was written in 1830, and was called " Missionary Success." It is as follows : —

> Hail to the brightness of Zion's glad morning !
> Joy to the lands that in darkness have lain !
> Hushed be the accents of sorrow and mourning ;
> Zion in triumph begins her mild reign.
>
> Hail to the brightness of Zion's glad morning,
> Long by the prophets of Israel foretold ;
> Hail to the millions from bondage returning ;
> Gentile and Jew the blest vision behold.
>
> Lo ! in the desert rich flowers are springing ;
> Streams ever copious are gliding along ;
> Loud from the mountain-tops echoes are ringing ;
> Wastes rise in verdure, and mingle in song.
>
> See from all lands—from the isles of the ocean—
> Praise of Jehovah ascending on high ;
> Fallen are the engines of war and commotion ;
> Shouts of salvation are rending the sky.

"My Times Are in Thy Hand"
William Freeman Lloyd

THIS New Year's hymn was written by William
Freeman Lloyd, who lived in England a
century ago. He was born in Gloucestershire, December 22, 1791. Sunday-school work attracted
him, and he taught classes in the college town of
Oxford and in London itself. It meant much to be
a Sunday-school teacher in those early days of the
Sunday school.

Mr. Lloyd was so active and successful in this
work that in 1810 he was made one of the secretaries
of the British Sunday School Union, and labored in
that important field for many years. He died in
Gloucestershire on April 22, 1853.

Besides the hymn given below, Mr. Lloyd wrote
one other that is in common use, "Wait, my soul,
upon the Lord," with its refrain, "As thy days thy
strength shall be." Our hymn was written in 1838,
and here are its five stanzas : —

> My times are in Thy hand ;
>   My God, I wish them there ;
> My life, my friends, my soul I leave
>   Entirely to Thy care.

> My times are in Thy hand,
>   Whatever they may be ;
> Pleasing or painful, dark or bright,
>   As best may seem to Thee.

My times are in Thy hand;
　Why should I doubt or fear?
My father's hand will never cause
　His child a needless tear.

My times are in Thy hand,
　Jesus, the crucified!
Those hands my cruel sins had pierced
　Are now my guard and guide.

My times are in Thy hand,
　I'll always trust in Thee;
And, after death, at Thy right hand
　I shall forever be.

"We Plough the Fields"

Matthias Claudius

THIS thanksgiving hymn was written by a German, Matthias Claudius, who was born in 1740. Though he was the son of a Lutheran minister and began to study to be a minister himself, he turned to the study of the law and came to lose much of his belief in religion. This tendency was furthered by his acquaintance with the great poet Goethe.

In 1779, however, Claudius had a severe illness, in the course of which he came to see his folly, and from that time he was a humble, sweet-spirited Christian, reflecting his faith in the poems he wrote. For the most part he spent his life as an editor of newspapers, and he contributed most of his beautiful poems to various periodicals. He died in Hamburg in 1815.

The only one of his hymns that has been translated into English and has been widely used is the one given below. It is part of a much longer poem that formed part of a sketch of country life, in the course of which the country people sang a harvest song. The translation most commonly used is by Miss Jane Montgomery Campbell, the daughter of an English clergyman. It is as follows:—

343

We plough the fields, and scatter
　The good seed on the land,
But it is fed and watered
　By God's almighty hand ;
He sends the snow in winter,
　The warmth to swell the grain,
The breezes and the sunshine,
　And soft, refreshing rain.

Refrain :

All good gifts around us
　Are sent from heaven above ;
Then thank the Lord, oh, thank the Lord,
　For all His love.

He only is the Maker
　Of all things near and far ;
He paints the wayside flower,
　He lights the evening star ;
The winds and waves obey Him ;
　By Him the birds are fed ;
Much more to us, His children,
　He gives our daily bread.

We thank Thee, then, O Father,
　For all things bright and good :
The seed-time and the harvest,
　Our life, our health, our food ;
Accept the gifts we offer
　For all Thy love imparts,
And, what Thou most desirest,
　Our humble, thankful hearts.

"Oh, Still in Accents Sweet and Strong"
Samuel Longfellow

SAMUEL LONGFELLOW was a brother of the famous poet, Henry Wadsworth Longfellow. He was a younger brother, having been born on June 18, 1819, twelve years after his brother Henry. Both were born in Portland, Me., and Samuel died there on October 3, 1892.

Samuel Longfellow was a Unitarian clergyman, and after graduating from Harvard University he became pastor of churches in Fall River, Mass., Brooklyn, N. Y., and Germantown, Penn. He was not only a writer of hymns but a compiler of hymn-books. At one time, with Samuel Johnson, of Boston, he was preparing a hymn-book and was at a loss for a good title. "Why," said a friend, referring to the Christian names of both the editors, "you might call it ' The Sam Book ! ' "

It was Samuel Longfellow who wrote the biography of his great brother. We also owe to him the establishing of what is known as "the vesper service" in the form in which so many churches now use it, —a most helpful institution.

Mr. Longfellow wrote many beautiful hymns, which have been used by the churches of all denominations. Among the finest of these is the hymn given below. It was first published in 1864.

345

Though not written as a missionary hymn, it is often
used for that purpose.

> Oh, still in accents sweet and strong
>   Sounds forth the ancient word,
> " More reapers for white harvest fields,
>   More laborers for the Lord."
>
> We hear the call; in dreams no more
>   In selfish ease we lie,
> But, girded for our Father's work,
>   Go forth beneath His sky.
>
> Where prophets' word, and martyrs' blood,
>   And prayers of saints were sown,
> We, to their labors entering in,
>   Would reap where they have strown.
>
> O Thou whose call our hearts has stirred,
>   To do Thy will we come;
> Thrust in our sickles at Thy word,
>   And bear our harvest home.

"The Spacious Firmament on High"

Joseph Addison

JOSEPH ADDISON was the greatest English
writer of his time, and one of the greatest of all
time. He was born May 1, 1672, at Milston, in the
County of Wiltshire, England. His father was the
Dean of Litchfield, and his mother was the sister of
the Bishop of Bristol, so that it is no wonder that the
boy was intended by his parents for the gospel ministry. However, he preferred the study of law and
politics, and became an influential public man.

After completing his studies at Oxford, he filled in
succession a number of important government offices,
becoming under-secretary of state, and finally chief
secretary for Ireland. King William III. gave him
a pension. He married Charlotte, the Dowager
Countess of Warwick. That was in 1716, and three
years later he came to an untimely end from asthma
and dropsy, passing away on June 17, 1719. His
body lay in state in the Jerusalem Chamber of Westminster Abbey, where the revision of the Bible was
made in the last years of the last century.

Addison was a man of unblemished character,
loved and admired by all. The poet Young says
that when he was dying he sent for the Earl of Warwick and said to him, "See in what peace a Christian can die !"

Addison wrote a very noble tragedy, "Cato," but

347

his greatest work was in prose. With his friend, Sir Richard Steele, he established *The Spectator*, a weekly paper consisting of an essay by himself or Steele or one of their friends—the beginning of the modern magazine and editorial. After this paper had run its course he established in succession *The Tatler*, *The Guardian*, and *The Freeholder*, writing for all of them a series of wonderful essays in the purest English, full of a wit and wisdom that have never been surpassed.

Five hymns, which are all that Addison is known to have written, were composed for *The Spectator*, and formed part of his essays there. One of these begins, "When all Thy mercies, O my God, my rising soul surveys." It was written after Addison's escape from shipwreck. Another, "How are Thy servants blessed, O Lord," is often called the travelers' hymn. It was probably written after his return from the same voyage. The others are, "When rising from the bed of death," "The Lord my pasture shall prepare," and the one given below, which is considered the finest of Addison's five hymns, and one of the finest in the English language.

It is Addison's version of Ps. 19, and it was published in *The Spectator*, No. 465, August 23, 1712. The hymn is often called "Creation," because it is sung to a selection from Haydn's great oratorio of that name. Here it is :—

> The spacious firmament on high,
> With all the blue etherial sky,
> And spangled heavens, a shining frame,
> Their great Original proclaim.

The unwearied sun from day to day
Does his Creator's power display,
And publishes to every land
The work of an almighty hand.

Soon as the evening shades prevail,
The moon takes up the wondrous tale,
And nightly to the listening earth
Repeats the story of her birth ;
Whilst all the stars that round her burn,
And all the planets in their turn,
Confirm the tidings as they roll,
And spread the truth from pole to pole.

What though in solemn silence all
Move round this dark terrestrial ball ;
What though no real voice nor sound
Amidst their radiant orbs be found,—
In reason's ear they all rejoice,
And utter forth a glorious voice,
Forever singing as they shine,
" The hand that made us is divine."

" When, Marshaled on the Nightly Plain "
Henry Kirke White

THIS is one of the most beautiful of Christmas poems. It was written by a remarkable young man, a poet who, like Keats and Chatterton, died at a very early age, before he had done more than give some hint of the power of genius that he possessed.

Henry Kirke White was born in Nottingham, England, March 21, 1785. His father was a butcher. His mother was a woman of ability, who, in order to get money to give her son the best possible education, opened a school for girls.

But the family were not able to send the boy to college, so he became, at the age of fourteen, a worker at a stocking-loom. He disliked this very much, and found an opportunity to study law.

He had not long engaged in this pursuit before he was converted. He had been surrounded by infidels, but one of them, a close friend of his, became converted, and began to avoid young White, knowing that he would be ridiculed and scorned. White inquired why his friend shunned him, and learned the reason. This set him to serious thinking, and at last he became a very earnest Christian.

So earnest was he that he determined to enter the gospel ministry. By this time his conspicuous abilities had won for him some influential friends, among whom was Henry Martyn, who became so famous as a missionary to India and Persia. These obtained for him the means to attend St. John's College, Cambridge University, where he paid part of his expenses by manual labor.   He was there, however, only a year, standing in the first rank among his classmates.   But overstudy brought on consumption, and he died of that dread disease on Sunday, October 19, 1806, when he was only twenty-one years old.

Henry White was a mere boy when he disclosed his talents.   At the age of thirteen he wrote the poem, " To an Early Primrose."   At the age of fifteen he lectured for two and three-quarters hours, it is said, without any direct preparation, on the subject of " Genius."   At that same age he won a silver medal for a translation from the Latin of Horace, and also two globes for a description of an imaginary journey from London to Edinburgh.   His first volume of poems was published when he was seventeen years old.

So well known had he become that his untimely death caused great sorrow.   Robert Southey wrote about him in prose and Byron in poetry.   A tablet to his memory was even set up in the United States, in Cambridge, Massachusetts.   It was everywhere felt that the world had lost a life of rare promise.

White wrote ten hymns.   One of the most popular and beautiful, " Oft in sorrow, oft in woe," may have been his last hymn.   It was written on the back of a mathematical exercise.   Another very fine poem is " The Lord, our God, is full of might."   But the hymn that is best liked and most used is probably the lovely Christmas hymn here printed.

The hymn, written in 1804, was first published in 1812, under the title, " The Star of Bethlehem." It is said to have been written to picture the poet's own experience in his conversion. " Once on the raging seas I rode " in a " foundering bark " is White's view of his condition when he was an unbeliever. This understanding of the hymn will make it all the more precious to us.

When, marshaled on the nightly plain,
    The glittering host bestud the sky,
One star alone, of all the train,
    Can fix the sinner's wandering eye.
Hark ! hark ! to God the chorus breaks
    From every host, from every gem ;
But one alone the Saviour speaks —
    It is the Star of Bethlehem.

Once on the raging seas I rode ;
    The storm was loud, the night was dark ;
The ocean yawned, and rudely blowed
    The wind, that tossed my foundering bark ;
Deep horror then my vitals froze ;
    Death-struck, I ceased the tide to stem ;
When suddenly a star arose, —
    It was the Star of Bethlehem !

It was my guide, my light, my all ;
    It bade my dark forebodings cease,
And through the storm and danger's thrall
    It led me to the port of peace.
Now safely moored, my perils o'er,
    I'll sing, first in night's diadem,
For ever and for evermore,
    The Star, the Star of Bethlehem !

"Father, Whate'er of Earthly Bliss"

Anne Steele

ANNE STEELE was the first woman writer whose hymns came to be largely used in hymn-books, and she is the greatest hymn-writer of her denomination, the Baptist. She was born at Broughton, Hampshire, England, in 1716. Her father was William Steele, a timber merchant, who preached for sixty years, mostly without a salary, in the Baptist church at Broughton, and all her life Anne was his faithful assistant in his religious work.

Her mother died when she was only three years old. She joined the church at the age of fourteen. She was a very delicate child, threatened with consumption, and in 1835 she suffered a severe injury to her hip. For the greater part of her life, therefore, she was an invalid, confined for much of the time to her room, and even helpless upon her bed. And yet she kept her cheerful and helpful disposition.

The sorest trial of Anne Steele's life came when she was twenty-one. Robert Elscourt, a noble young man to whom she was engaged to be married, was drowned the day before their wedding was to take place. She never married, being in this respect, as in many others, quite like another great hymn-writer, Dr. Isaac Watts, who lived at a distance of only fifteen miles from her. This sad loss was undoubtedly in her mind as she wrote the hymn we have selected.

Miss Steele's poems did not appear in print until 1760, and then only under the pen-name of "Theodosia." She directed that the profits from the book should be spent in charity. Her father wrote in his diary: "This day Nanny sent part of her composition to London to be printed. I entreat a gracious God, who enabled and stirred her up to such a work, to direct in it and bless it for the good of many. I pray God to make it useful, and keep her humble." All parts of that prayer were certainly answered.

It is difficult for us to realize the tremendous popularity that attended these hymns. The wide use of some of "Fanny Crosby's" hymns of the present day is something like it. For example, in 1808 the Episcopal church in Boston that Phillips Brooks made famous, Trinity Church, printed its own hymn-book. It consisted of 152 hymns, and 59 of these were Miss Steele's. In all, Miss Steele wrote 144 hymns, and 34 Psalms in verse. Many of these are still sung, including " Dear Refuge of my weary soul," "My God, my Father, blissful name," " He lives, the great Redeemer lives," " Alas! what hourly dangers rise," and " Father of Mercies, in Thy Word." Her hymns are very simple, clear, and beautiful, breathing a spirit of Christian faith and resignation.

Of all her hymns, doubtless the following is the favorite :—

> Father, whate'er of earthly bliss
>   Thy sovereign will denies,
> Accepted at Thy throne, let this
>   My humble prayer, arise :
>
> Give me a calm and thankful heart,
>   From every murmur free ;
> The blessings of Thy grace impart,
>   And make me live to Thee.
>
> Let the sweet hope that Thou are mine
>   My life and death attend,
> Thy presence through my journey shine,
>   And crown my journey's end.

This hymn is taken from a poem of ten stanzas entitled " Desiring Resignation and Thankfulness." The hymn is the last three stanzas, and the choice was made by Toplady, the author of " Rock of Ages." The first line of the original poem is " When I survey life's varied scenes." " Naomi," the lovely tune always used with this hymn, was written expressly for it by Lowell Mason, in 1836.

It may be asked how the last line of the hymn, referring to " the journey's end," was carried out in life. Very beautifully indeed, for this is the account of her death : " She took the most affectionate leave of her weeping friends around her ; and at length, the happy moment of her dismission arriving, she closed her eyes, and with these animating words on her dying lips, 'I know that my Redeemer liveth,' gently fell asleep in Jesus."

That was in November, 1778.   Her body was laid away in Broughton church-yard, and on her tomb-stone are these words :—

> Silent the lyre, and dumb the tuneful tongue,
>   That sung on earth her great Redeemer's praise ;
> But now in heaven she joins the angelic song,
>   In more harmonious, more exalted lays.

"More Love to Thee, O Christ"

Elizabeth Payson Prentiss

ELIZABETH PAYSON was the youngest daughter of Dr. Edward Payson, a famous and very devout clergyman of Portland, Me. When she was very young she began to write both prose and verse, and contributed to *The Youth's Companion* when she was only sixteen. She became a pious and beautiful young woman, with a finely trained mind. As a teacher in Portland, in Ipswich, Mass., and in Richmond, Va., she was greatly beloved.

In 1845 she married Rev. George L. Prentiss, D. D., who became a professor in Union Theological Seminary, New York City. In 1869 appeared her most famous story, "Stepping Heavenward," more than 200,000 copies of which have been sold in the United States, while many translations have been printed in other parts of the world. "The Flower of the Family" is another of Mrs. Prentiss's stories that has been widely read.

As a poet, Mrs. Prentiss is best known by the beautiful hymn which we give here. It was written probably in 1856, in a time of great sorrow for her. It was little regarded at the time, and it was thirteen years before Mrs. Prentiss thought to show it to her husband. Then, in 1869, the hymn was printed on a slip of paper for private distribution. The next year came the great revival, and the hymn sprang into wide popularity.

"More love to Thee, O Christ," has been translated into many languages and sung all over the earth. When the Chinese heard of Mrs. Prentiss's death, in 1878, they wrote the hymn in Chinese characters upon a fan, which they sent to Dr. Prentiss.

> More love to Thee, O Christ,
>   More love to Thee!
> Hear Thou the prayer I make
>   On bended knee;
> This is my earnest plea,
> More love, O Christ, to Thee,
>   More love to Thee!
>
> Once earthly joy I craved,
>   Sought peace and rest;
> Now Thee alone I seek,
>   Give what is best;
> This all my prayer shall be,
> More love, O Christ, to Thee,
>   More love to Thee!
>
> Let sorrow do its work,
>   Send grief and pain;
> Sweet are Thy messengers,
>   Sweet their refrain,
> When they can sing with me,
> More love, O Christ, to Thee,
>   More love to Thee!

Then shall my latest breath
  Whisper Thy praise ;
This be the parting cry
  My heart shall raise,
This still its prayer shall be,
More love, O Christ, to Thee,
  More love to Thee !

"As Shadows Cast by Cloud and Sun "
William Cullen Bryant

WILLIAM CULLEN BRYANT, the author of this hymn, was the first of the great American poets. He was the son of a physician, and was born at Cummington, Mass., November 3, 1794. He was éducated in Williams College, and as a lawyer. He became an editor in New York City, where he founded *The New York Review*, and edited *The New York Evening Post*.

Bryant was only a young man when he wrote "Thanatopsis," which at once made him famous. He lived a long and honored life, dying in his eighty-fourth year, June 12, 1878. He passed away at his country home on Long Island, being killed by a fall which came as he was weary after delivering an oration in the open air at Central Park.

Bryant wrote more than twenty hymns, but only two or three of them are in common use. The best known is the noble home-missionary hymn, "Look from Thy sphere of endless day." The Christmas hymn here printed was written for the semi-centennial of the Church of the Messiah in Boston, March 19, 1875. It was sung at the poet's funeral. Note how suitable the hymn is to that occasion, as well as to the occasion for which it was written, and also to our Christmas and New Year seasons. Here are the verses :—

As shadows cast by cloud and sun
   Flit o'er the summer grass,
So, in Thy sight, Almighty One,
   Earth's generations pass.
And as the years, an endless host,
   Come swiftly pressing on,
The brightest names that earth can boast
   Just glisten and are gone.

Yet doth the star of Bethlehem shed
   A lustre pure and sweet;
And still it leads, as once it led,
   To the Messiah's feet.
O Father, may that holy star
   Grow every year more bright,
And send its glorious beams afar
   To fill the world with light.

"The King of Love My Shepherd Is"
Henry Williams Baker

ONE of the most beautiful hymns ever written is the one beginning, "The King of love my Shepherd is." This hymn was written by Sir Henry Williams Baker, Bart., who was the eldest son of Sir Henry Loraine Baker, an admiral in the British navy. The poet was born in London, May 27, 1821.

After his graduation from the Universiy of Cambridge he became a clergyman of the Church of England, becoming vicar of Monkland in Herefordshire, and occupied that position until his death on February 12, 1877.

He edited hymnals and devotional books, but is best known for the few very fine hymns that he himself composed. One of his first hymns is, "Oh, what if we are Christ's?" He wrote thirty-three hymns, all of them simple and earnest and smoothly flowing. Most of them are tender and plaintive, or even sad. His last words were from his own hymn, the one given below, the stanza beginning, "Perverse and foolish, oft I strayed." This hymn is, of course, based upon the Twenty-third Psalm, and it is as follows : —

> The King of love my Shepherd is,
>   Whose goodness faileth never :
> I nothing lack if I am His
>   And He is mine forever.

Where streams of living water flow
  My ransomed soul He leadeth,
And, where the verdant pastures grow,
  With food celestial feedeth.

Perverse and foolish, oft I strayed,
  But yet in love He sought me,
And on His shoulder gently laid,
  And home, rejoicing, brought me.

In death's dark vale I fear no ill
  With Thee, dear Lord, beside me;
Thy rod and staff my comfort still,
  Thy cross before to guide me.

Thou spread'st a table in my sight;
  Thy unction grace bestoweth;
And oh, what transport of delight
  From Thy pure chalice floweth!

And so through all the length of days,
  Thy goodness faileth never:
Good Shepherd, may I sing Thy praise
  Within Thy house forever.

"Prayer Is the Soul's Sincere Desire"

James Montgomery

MOST of the great hymn-writers have been
ministers, but the author of this fine hymn
was a layman,—James Montgomery. He and William Cowper stand at the head of the laymen who
have written hymns (lay*women* not being taken into
account!) and the hymns of no other layman are
found in so great numbers in our hymn-books.

Montgomery was born at Irvine, in Ayrshire,
Scotland (the region in which Robert Burns was
born), November 4, 1771. His parents were Moravian missionaries, and both of them went to the
West Indies in 1783, where they died soon afterward. The lad became apprentice to a grocer,
from whom he ran away. He tried to get his
poems printed in London, for he had already begun
to write, but in this he failed. At last he became
assistant to the publisher of a newspaper in Sheffield.
This paper was opposed to the government, and its
publisher finally went away to America to avoid
prosecution for his utterances.

Upon this, Montgomery took entire charge of the
paper, renamed it *The Sheffield Iris,* and conducted
it for thirty-one years. During the first two years
of his life as an editor Montgomery was put in
prison twice by the government, once for reprinting

a poem favorable to the French Revolution, and once for giving an account of a riot in Sheffield. He gave up his newspaper work in 1825, and in 1833 the government made amends for his imprisonment by bestowing upon him a pension of a thousand dollars a year. He had become a famous writer, and was greatly loved. When he died, in his sleep, April 30, 1854, Sheffield gave him a public funeral, and erected in his honor a bronze statue.

Montgomery wrote a number of long poems, but they are not read now. Near the end of the poet's life a friend asked him, "Which of your poems will live?" He answered, "None, sir; nothing, except perhaps a few of my hymns." That judgment was correct, except that more than "a few" of the hymns have survived. He wrote about four hundred hymns, and of these about one hundred are still in common use.

It would be difficult to say which of his hymns is the favorite. Some would vote for "Jerusalem, my happy home." Others would prefer the magnificent hymn, "Hail to the Lord's anointed." Montgomery was a missionary enthusiast, as the son of such parents surely should have been. He gave many missionary addresses, and wrote other great missionary hymns, among them "Hark! the song of jubilee."

Another favorite is his "Sow in the morn thy seed," which was written for the Sunday-school children of Sheffield, and sung every year for twenty-five years by a gathering of twenty thousand of them. Still other splendid hymns of his are "The Lord is my Shepherd, no want shall I know,"

"Call Jehovah thy salvation," "Forever with the Lord," "Oh, where shall rest be found?" "Holy, holy, holy Lord," "To Thy temple I repair," "Songs of praise the angels sang," "Angels, from the realms of glory," "Go to dark Gethsemane," "In the hour of trial," "What are these in bright array?" and many others almost equally famous.

There are a large number of Christians, however, whose choice among all Montgomery's hymns would be the noble poem on prayer given below, the most perfect definition of prayer in all poetry. Montgomery said that he had received more praise for this hymn than for anything else he had ever written. The poet's last words were words of prayer. He had been conducting family prayers, and had offered, a prayer in which he had poured out his whole soul. Immediately afterward he went to bed, and passed away that night in his sleep. Thus he "entered heaven with prayer."

> Prayer is the soul's sincere desire,
>   Uttered or unexpressed ;
> The motion of a hidden fire
>   That trembles in the breast.
>
> Prayer is the burden of a sigh,
>   The falling of a tear,
> The upward glancing of an eye,
>   When none but God is near.
>
> Prayer is the simplest form of speech
>   That infant lips can try ;
> Prayer the sublimest strains that reach
>   The Majesty on high.

Prayer is the Christian's vital breath,
  The Christian's native air,
His watchword at the gates of death —
  He enters heaven with prayer.

Prayer is the contrite sinner's voice,
  Returning from his ways;
While angels in their songs rejoice,
  And cry, "Behold, he prays!"

O Thou, by whom we come to God,
  The Life, the Truth, the Way,
The path of prayer Thyself hast trod;
  Lord, teach us how to pray.

"Thy Way, Not Mine, O Lord"
Horatius Bonar

HORATIUS BONAR, who wrote this hymn, was one of the noblest of the many noble souls that Scotland has produced. He was born in Edinburgh, December 19, 1808, and became the minister at Kelso. When the Scottish Presbyterian Church was split in 1843, he went with the other leaders of the Church into the Free Church of Scotland, and remained in that denomination, preaching chiefly in Edinburgh, till his death in 1889. His brother was the Bible commentator, Dr. Andrew A. Bonar. His greatest teacher was the famous Christian leader, Dr. Thomas Chalmers.

Dr. Bonar wrote many poems, and nearly one hundred of his lovely hymns have come into common use. Most of these songs were written for his Sunday school, and were sung there. His denomination used only the Psalms, and it was not until near the close of his life that Dr. Bonar introduced his hymns into the services of his own church. When he did, two of his elders rose and walked indignantly out of the building.

The author himself thought that his best hymn was " When the weary seeking rest." Perhaps the favorite of most persons is " I heard the voice of Jesus say." Among other beautiful hymns by Dr. Bonar are " Beyond the smiling and the weeping," " Go,

labor on ; spend and be spent," " Yes, for me, for me
He careth," " A few more years shall roll," " I was a
wandering sheep," " I see the crowd in Pilate's hall,"
and " I lay my sins on Jesus." He was a man of a
tender, loving, peaceful spirit, and his hymns perfectly represent his character.

Many of Dr. Bonar's hymns were published for the
first time in the three series of " Hymns of Faith and
Hope." The hymn here given, though it appeared,
according to Duffield, in 1856, was printed in the
first series of the " Hymns of Faith and Hope,"
which was published in 1857. It had seven stanzas
there, and these are given below. As it is sung in
stanzas of eight lines each, however, the second of
these stanzas is omitted from our hymn-books.

> Thy way, not mine, O Lord,
>   However dark it be !
> Lead me by Thine own hand ;
>   Choose out the path for me.
>
> Smooth let it be or rough,
>   It will be still the best ;
> Winding or straight, it matters not,
>   It leads me to Thy rest.
>
> I dare not choose my lot :
>   I would not, if I might ;
> Choose Thou for me, my God ;
>   So shall I walk aright.
>
> The kingdom that I seek
>   Is Thine : so let the way
> That leads to it be Thine,
>   Else I must surely stray.

Take Thou my cup, and it
  With joy or sorrow fill,
As best to Thee may seem ;
  Choose Thou my good and ill.

Choose Thou for me my friends,
  My sickness or my health ;
Choose Thou my cares for me,
  My poverty or wealth.

Not mine, not mine the choice,
  In things or great or small ;
Be Thou my guide, my strength,
  My wisdom, and my all.

"Hark! Ten Thousand Harps and Voices"
Thomas Kelly

THOMAS KELLY, who wrote this hymn, was born July 13, 1769, in Kellyville, near Athy, Ireland. His father was a judge of the Irish Court of Common Pleas, and educated his son at Trinity College, Dublin, intending him for the law. He was a friend of Edmund Burke, and would probably have made a success of the law, but he was led to study Hebrew, and from that study he came to prefer the work of a minister. He grew to be very earnest in religion, and endangered his health by the severity of his devoutness.

He was at first a clergyman of the Church of England, but his preaching was too vigorous for the times, and his archbishop forbade him to preach in any of the churches of the diocese; therefore he became an independent, and founded a number of churches of his own. At the age of thirty he married a lady of most congenial disposition and considerable wealth. He labored zealously till his eighty-fifth year, when on May 14, 1854, he died from a stroke of paralysis. As he lay dying some one repeated, "The Lord is my shepherd." At once he replied, "The Lord is my *everything*." His last words were, "Not my will, but Thine, be done."

Mr. Kelly published several volumes of hymns, and wrote 765 in all. Of those that have come into

common use the best known are : " On the mountain-
top appearing," "In Thy name, O Lord, assembling,"
" Look, ye saints ; the sight is glorious," " The head
that once was crowned with thorns," " The people of
the Lord are on their way to heaven," " Saviour,
through the desert lead us," " What is life ? 'tis but
a vapor," " Sons of Zion, raise your songs."

Probably Mr. Kelly's most famous hymn is the one
given below.   It was published in 1806, and is therefore more than a century old.   It was printed at first
with the text, " Let all the angels of God worship
him," standing at its head.   Originally written in
seven stanzas of six lines each, it is now always
printed in a condensed form, as follows : —

> Hark ! ten thousand harps and voices
>   Sound the notes of praise above ;
> Jesus reigns, and heaven rejoices ;
>   Jesus reigns, the God of love.
> See, He sits on yonder throne ;
> Jesus rules the world alone.
>
> Jesus, hail ! whose glory brightens
>   All above, and gives it worth ;
> Lord of life, Thy smile enlightens,
>   Cheers, and charms Thy sons of earth :
> When we think of love like Thine,
> Lord, we own it love divine.
>
> King of glory, reign forever ;
>   Thine an everlasting crown ;
> Nothing from Thy love shall sever
>   Those whom Thou hast made Thine own ;
> Happy objects of Thy grace,
> Destined to behold Thy face.

Saviour, hasten Thine appearing ;
   Bring, O bring the glorious day,
When, the awful summons hearing,
   Heaven and earth shall pass away:
Then with golden harps we'll sing
Glory, glory to our King.

" Fight the Good Fight "
John Samuel Bewley Monsell

THIS stirring hymn was written by John Samuel
Bewley Monsell, LL. D., who was born at St.
Columb's, Londonderry, Ireland, March 2, 1811.
His father, the archdeacon of Londonderry, educated the boy at Trinity College, Dublin, and he
became a clergyman of the Church of England. He
died on April 9, 1875, at Guildford, England, where
he fell from the roof of his church which was being
rebuilt.

Dr. Monsell published no fewer than eleven volumes of hymns ; in these, however, there are many
repetitions, so that the total number of hymns that
he wrote is about 300. Of these a very large number, about one-fourth, are in common use, including
" God is love, that anthem olden," " Sing to the
Lord a joyful song," " Light of the world, we hail
Thee," " Rest of the weary, joy of the sad," " Holy
offerings, rich and rare," " On our way rejoicing,"
" Worship the Lord in the beauty of holiness," " O'er
the distant mountains breaking," " To Thee, O dear,
dear Saviour." All of Dr. Monsell's hymns are
musical and full of beauty and expression.

The hymn we have selected was first printed in
1863, and was entitled "The Fight of Faith." Its
four stanzas are as follows : —

Fight the good fight with all thy might ;
Christ is thy strength and Christ thy right ;
Lay hold on life, and it shall be
Thy joy and crown eternally.

Run the straight race through God's good grace ;
Lift up thine eyes, and seek His face ;
Life with its way before us lies ;
Christ is the path and Christ the prize.

Cast care aside, upon thy Guide
Lean, and His mercy will provide ;
Lean, and the trusting soul shall prove
Christ is its life and Christ its love.

Faint not, nor fear ; His arms are near ;
He changeth not, and thou art dear ;
Only believe, and thou shalt see
That Christ is all in all to thee.

" Lead, Kindly Light "

John Henry Newman

JOHN HENRY NEWMAN was the son of John
Newman, a London banker, and was born on
February 21, 1801. He was a very superstitious
boy, and used to cross himself often when he went
into dark places. He was converted at the age of
fifteen and became filled with a sense of the nearness
of God, a feeling which remained with him all his
life. At that time he made up his mind that it was
God's will that he should never marry.

Newman was graduated from Trinity College,
Oxford, in 1820, and remained there to study and
teach. In 1824 he became a clergyman of the
Church of England, and at once began to preach in
a very wonderful and powerful way. It was at this
time that Newman, who had been strongly opposed
to the Roman Catholic Church, began to admire it,
to think of the Protestant Reformation as a mistake,
and to believe the Catholic superstitions of the real
presence of Christ's body in the bread and wine of
the communion and the worship of the Virgin Mary.

All this time, however, Newman had no thought
of becoming a Catholic, but he was deeply grieved
at the progress made by the liberal party in the
English Church. Suffering from poor health he

journeyed to Italy, met Catholics in Rome, and went down alone to Sicily, where he was sick with a fever and his servant thought he was dying. At last he grew better and set off across the Mediterranean for Marseilles. It was on this voyage, on June 16, 1833, that he wrote our hymn, " Lead, Kindly Light." The great hymn, therefore, was not the product of a Catholic, but of a clergyman of the Church of England, who was greatly distressed, who felt that things were going wrong, and who was torn by the feeling that he himself ought to do something to set them right. It was his prayer for leading in his perplexity, and has become the prayer for guidance of many million saints.

But, alas ! Newman followed the poor wax candle of Catholicism rather than the Light of the World. In 1845, twelve years after writing this hymn, he joined the Catholic Church, and served it so faithfully that in 1879 he was made a cardinal. He wrote many able books, including a defence of his life, called " Apologia pro Vita Suo," and he lived to old age, dying in 1890. Though he erred greatly in leaving the true principles of Protestantism, he was a sincere man of pure and beautiful spirit and of deep religious feeling. His great hymn could hardly come from a different source.

The hymn was first printed in *The British Magazine* in March, 1834, with the title, " Faith-Heavenly Leadings." In 1836 he printed it with the title, " Light in the Darkness," and the motto, " Unto the godly there ariseth up light in the darkness." Still later he gave it the title, " The Pillar of the Cloud."

Newman himself modestly attributed the popularity of the hymn to the beautiful tune, " Lux Benigna," written for it by Dr. Dykes in 1865—a tune which the composer framed while walking through the Strand in London.

The " angel faces " in the last stanza of the hymn are often supposed to be the faces of loved ones gone before. Newman himself, however, after his conversion said that he was conscious of the presence of angels when awake and often in his sleep, but after a while he lost this sense of their presence and greatly grieved over the loss. It may be, therefore, that the poet expressed in this stanza the hope that these angel presences would return to him. Newman himself refused to throw light on this point.

The hymn, as Newman himself printed it, is as follows :—

Lead, kindly Light, amid the encircling gloom,
　　Lead Thou me on ;
The night is dark, and I am far from home ;
　　Lead Thou me on :
Keep Thou my feet ; I do not ask to see
The distant scene,—one step enough for me.

I was not ever thus, nor prayed that Thou
　　Shouldst lead me on :
I loved to choose and see my path ; but now
　　Lead Thou me on.
I loved the garish day, and, spite of fears,
Pride ruled my will : remember not past years.

So long Thy power hath blest me, sure it still
    Will lead me on
O'er moor and fen, o'er crag and torrent, till
    The night is gone;
And with the morn those angel faces smile,
Which I have loved long since, and lost awhile.

" Pass It On "

Henry Burton

SEVENTY-THREE years ago Henry Burton was
born in a rambling old farm house at Swanning-
ton, in Leicestershire, England—a house where his
ancestors had lived for two centuries. He was born
in a family of deep piety, all being ardent Methodists.
His grandfather was class leader. His grandmother
in 1814 founded the first Methodist juvenile missionary society. Morning and evening prayers were
regularly observed in his father's house.

Always a follower of Christ, young Henry made
his first public avowal at the age of fifteen in his
father's barn, where services were being held while
the chapel was being enlarged. At once he began
to teach in the Sunday school, though only the
youngest children.

In 1856 the family—father, mother, and ten children—emigrated to America and went to a farm in
northern Illinois. Henry went to the academy of
Beloit College and finally graduated from the college
in 1862, having walked more than five thousand
miles to get his education.

When Henry was a mere boy his mother had paid
him a shilling to read the six volumes of Jackson's
" Lives of the Early Methodist Preachers,"—" an of-

fer," he writes, " which I gladly accepted, though not perhaps with the purest motive."

On his graduation he became convinced that he ought to preach, and three days after graduating he was on his way to supply the pulpit of the brother of Frances Willard, whose health had broken down for the time. Then he supplied at Monroe, Wis., for a church whose pastor had gone to the war as chaplain, and under his ministry there came a wonderful revival, with services every evening, except Saturdays, for six weeks, and with fifty new members added to the church, chiefly adults. The strain and excitement of this work so injured Mr. Burton's health that he went to England, whither his family had already gone. There for many years he has labored, completing forty-one years in the pastorate, though three of these years were spent in a severe sickness, when his life was despaired of by eight doctors.

The degree of doctor of divinity has been bestowed upon him most fittingly. He married the daughter of Mark Guy Pearse, the sister of Rev. Mark Guy Pearse, the famous London preacher. Three of their seven children have become ministers.

Dr. Burton wrote the commentary on Luke in " The Expositor's Bible," and has done other important literary work, but he is best known for his hymns. Among them are " O King of Kings," which was written at the request of Sir John Stainer, the composer ; " Break, Day of God " ; " Hymn for the Sea," (which is placed in all the Cunarders and lightships, and sung at the Sunday services of all the vessels of the White Star Line); the missionary hymn, " There's a Light upon the Mountains " ; and " Epworth," the hymn of the Wesley Guild.

But of all his hymns the most famous, certainly in America, is " Pass It On," regarding which I have been favored with the following account from Dr. Burton himself :

" The incident which gave rise to the song was an experience of the Rev. Mark Guy Pearse, who is my brother-in-law ; and I give it now in Mr. Pearse's own words. ' Once when I was a schoolboy going home from the far-away little town in which I dwelt (Zeist, Holland) I arrived at Bristol, and got on board the steamer with just enough money to pay my fare ; and that being settled, I thought in my innocence that I had paid for everything in the way of meals. I had what I wanted as long as we were in smooth water ; then came the rough Atlantic, and the need of noth- ing more. I had been lying in my berth for hours wretchedly ill, and past caring for anything when the steward came and stood beside me.

" ' Your bill, sir,' said he, holding out a piece of paper.

" ' I have no money,' said I, in my wretchedness.

" ' Then I shall keep your luggage. What is your name and address ? ' I told him. Instantly he took off the cap he wore, with the gilt band around it, and held out his hand. ' I should like to shake hands with you,' he said. Then came the explanation— how that, some years before, a little kindness had been shown his mother by my father in the sorrow of her widowhood. ' I never thought the chance would come for me to repay it,' he said pleasantly, 'but I'm glad it has.' As soon as I got ashore I told my father what had happened. ' Ah,' said he, ' see how a bit of kindness lives ! Now he has passed it on to you ; and remember, if you meet anybody who needs a friendly hand, you must pass it on to him.'

" Such is the simple incident, which I first heard from the lips of my father-in-law, Mr. Mark Guy Pearse, of London, and it was his ' Pass it on ' which gave the inspiration and the title to my little song.

" The words have had, to my knowledge, some sixteen different musical settings, but the most popular one in England is the one composed by your own Mr. George C. Stebbins, which has been sung by Gipsy Smith all round the world."

This hymn was written, as Dr. Burton tells me, on April 3, 1885, and the following is the entire poem as the author has copied it for me. In our hymnals the third stanza is usually omitted : —

> Have you had a kindness shown?
>   Pass it on !
> 'Twas not given for thee alone —
>   Pass it on !
> Let it travel down the years,
> Let it wipe another's tears,
> Till in heaven the deed appears,
>   Pass it on !
>
> Did you hear the loving word —
>   Pass it on !
> Like the singing of a bird ?
>   Pass it on !

Let its music live and grow,
Let it cheer another's woe,
You have reaped what others sow —
        Pass it on !

'Twas the sunshine of a smile —
        Pass it on !
Staying but a little while ?
        Pass it on !
April beam, the little thing,
Still it wakes the flowers of spring,
Makes the silent birds to sing —
        Pass it on !

Have you found the heavenly light ?
        Pass it on !
Souls are groping in the night,
        Daylight gone ;
Hold thy lighted lamp on high,
Be a star in some one's sky,
He may live who else would die —
        Pass it on !

Love demands the loving deed ;
        Pass it on !
Look upon thy brother's need,
        Pass it on !
Live for self, you live in vain ;
Live for Christ, you live again ;
Live for Him, with Him you reign —
        Pass it on !

Index of Titles

Index of Authors